What people are saying about *Dreaming in 3D* . . .

"Doug used to take me to Pizza Hut when I was a kid, so I've always known he's a fun guy. In the 30 years since I was a boy, I've learned that he brings an energy and enthusiasm to life that is truly rare. I've been fortunate to have a front row seat to watch one of the most creative, inspiring, strategic leaders I've ever known. I believe his words will ignite your dreams. They sure have fueled mine."
—Brad Leach, Pastor of CityLife Church, South Philadelphia, Pennsylvania

"Not every dreamer knows how to see their dreams come true. Doug's book, *Dreaming in 3D*, will not only inspire you to capture God's dream for your life, but will provide you a road map to start following that dream."
—Gabby Mejia, Pastor of New Birth, Orlando, Florida

"God's dream isn't easy, but it's always meaningful. *Dreaming in 3D* brings into clear focus the power of a dream. It helps you see the critical process in fulfilling God's purposes for your life. It has been my privilege to see Doug Clay pursue his dreams with a passion for God, a heart for people and a commitment to integrity. I am confident that this book will be a valuable resource in helping many to discover and realize the dreams that God has for them. Start reading and dream!"
—Chad Gilligan, Pastor of Calvary, Toledo, Ohio

"In working with Doug on a professional level, it is obvious that he is driven by a clear dream and is living life with a purpose. In fact, he lives his life in 3E: enthusiastically, energetically, and excitingly! His ideas and messages are always very motivational and inspirational to me. I am confident that *Dreaming in 3D* will start you on your path of chasing your dreams!"
—Daniel C Burns, Co-owner, Employee Benefit Design, LLC

This book is dedicated to Rev. Arthur G. Clay (1930–1972), whose memory and legacy has inspired me to dream.

Contents

Acknowledgements

I want to express my deep appreciation to those who have affected my life's journey and whose significant contributions have motivated the writing of this book.

To Gail, the wife of my dreams, whose unwavering support gives me the strength to meet each day.

To my girls, Ashley and Kaylee, who have helped me to dream in living color, and have been a great source of love and laughter.

To my mother, Audrey Clay, the greatest dream-releaser I know, who provides relentless determination to help her children, and others, chase their dreams.

To Bill Leach, a godly mentor, who as a father-figure in my life, helps me to keep the dream in focus.

To Gary Meyer, whose life and friendship inspires me to keep dreaming.

To Pat Springle, a gifted writer, who, with the stroke of a pen, can make dreams come true.

To Calvary Assembly of God in Toledo, Ohio and the Ohio Ministry Network. In these ministry opportunities, dreams became realities.

To the Division of Treasury's management team, who share the dream of being a premier service agency of the Assemblies of God.

To my Heavenly Father, whose dreams for us are worth a lifelong pursuit.

Foreword

I've seen it firsthand. Doug Clay lives a blessed life. He was blessed by a determined, hard-working mother who, with the help of a great church, coached young Doug through the untimely death of his father. He is continually blessed by the benefits that come from the discipline of applying the Word of God in daily decisions and from choosing to avoid cutting corners or straying from the faith. And he is blessed by the unrelenting resolve to trust that God has plans to prosper believers in all areas of their lives, regardless of the steep challenges they may be facing.

I vividly remember accompanying Doug to the Far East on one of his dreams. The leadership structure and ministry scope he had in mind for missions work had not yet been attempted in our circles. Through the relentless humidity and hard labor, Doug forged ahead with the daunting challenge of relationship-building, resource-raising, and paradigm-shifting necessary for his God-inspired dream to become reality. Looking back now, the headline for his work could have been: "Dream Accomplished for God's Glory." Reading *Dreaming in 3D* reinforces for me the behind-the-scenes building blocks that were so critical to Doug's success—then and now.

As a longtime friend and co-worker, I'm thrilled for Doug's readers and admirers to have this book in your hands. You will gain valuable insights into his personal story, one that I am not alone in characterizing as anointed leadership and effective ministry. But more importantly, the powerful combination of quotes and illustrations will make the case for the dreams that will impact your life today. Get ready to believe in your future!

In this highly motivational and well grounded work, Doug outlines heaven's never-ending plan to see us all become the divinely designed masterpieces God intended, and he reveals scriptural truths in meaningful context that readers of all ages will find intriguing and relevant. Prepare yourself to count the times you say, "I never saw that passage like that before!"

Dreaming in 3D is a manifesto for any Spirit-driven Christian. When we get to heaven, we won't be dreaming any more. Until then, God-inspired dreams should be a regular expectation and experience of all God's children. Doug has taken the time and care like few others have to break down the components of properly stewarding the treasure trove of dreams delivered to each of us by the Spirit.

For people who are following God with all their hearts, this book provides additional insights and encouragement to "excel still more." For people living the nightmare of hopelessness, confusion, or lack of fulfillment, *Dreaming in 3D* will bring welcome and refreshing clarity. I heartily recommend this book to people who want to find and follow God's dream for their lives.

John Wootton
District Superintendent
Ohio Ministry Network

1 The Source of a Dream

The thing is to understand myself, to see what God really wants me to do;

the thing is to find a truth which is true for me, to find the idea for which

I can live and die.

—Søren Kierkegaard

People discover their dreams by discovering God. His creative work didn't stop when He finished the days of creation. He's still helping men and women of all ages uncover the most rewarding purpose life can offer. We aren't limited by our financial condition or family background. In fact, God delights in overcoming obstacles and fulfilling the dreams of people who might be passed over by others. The only raw materials we need to find and follow God's dream for our lives are faith and creativity. I believe God has incredible things for each one of us—if only we'll pursue Him passionately, listen carefully, and walk courageously in the direction He leads.

Too often, however, people live in the gray twilight of empty hearts and small (if any) dreams. Author Kenneth Hildebrand explained:

> *The poorest of all men is not the one without a nickel to his name. He is the fellow without a dream. . . . [He is like] a great ship made for*

the mighty ocean but trying to navigate in a millpond. He has no far port to reach, no lifting horizon no precious cargo to carry. His hours are absorbed in routine and petty tyrannies. Small wonder if he gets dissatisfied, quarrelsome, and "fed up." One of life's greatest tragedies is a person with a 10-by-12 capacity and a two-by-four soul.[1]

When I speak on the topic of dreaming in 3D, people sometimes ask, "Is it really possible to dream this way and experience the fulfillment of our dreams?" Yes, it certainly is. I'm confident of this answer because I've lived it. In fact, my life has surpassed my greatest dreams. My father died when I was nine years old, and my mother devoted herself to raise me. Both of my parents modeled a life of discovering and fulfilling God's dream for their lives. I watched carefully, and their example inspired me. As I often say about them, "They threw me a catchable pass." I missed my father terribly, but my mother never lost an opportunity to give me the support, encouragement, and direction that I needed in order to find myself, first as a boy and then as a young man. Today, my relationships with my wife, Gail, and our daughters, Ashley and Kaylee, are great delights to me, and the role God has given me challenges me to give my very best each day. I'm thrilled to be where I am, and I look forward to each day's joys and struggles because I know I'm living out God's dream for my life.

One of life's greatest tragedies is a person with a 10-by-12 capacity and a two-by-four soul.

No Carbon Copies

God's dream for me, though, isn't like His dream for anyone else. Oh, there are some similarities, but God doesn't use a cookie cutter when He designs our dreams. Each of us has a common calling to know and follow Christ, but beyond this universal invitation, God has carefully crafted each of us in certain ways for specific roles that no one else can fill. In his letter to the Christians in Ephesus, Paul wrote, "He creates each of us by Christ Jesus to join him in the work he does, the good work he has gotten ready for us to do, work we had better be doing" (Ephesians 2:10, *Message*). Another translation says that we are "God's masterpiece" (NLT), put on display for all to see. God created and crafted each of us for a divine and unique purpose. Our task—our high privilege and deep responsibility—is to uncover God's purpose for our lives, unpack the gifts and talents He has built into us, and then live each day in reckless abandon to His will. Rick Warren, best-selling author of *The Purpose Driven Life*, commented, "You were made *by* God and *for* God—and until you understand that, life will never make sense."[2]

In our culture, we compare almost everything: beauty, investments, cars, vacations, body shape, clothes, gadgets, and every other conceivable characteristic. But when we think about God's dream for us, we need to realize it's one of a kind, not one size fits all. Holocaust survivor Elie Wiesel observed, "When you die and go to heaven and you meet God, God is not going to say to you, 'Why didn't you become a saint? Why didn't you discover the cure for cancer? Why didn't you change the world?' No, all God will ask you at that holy time is, 'Why didn't you become you?'"[3] In a similar vein, the Danish theologian and philosopher Søren Kierkegaard reflected on God's plan for his life: "And now, with God's help, I shall become myself."[4] God's purpose isn't to bypass us, but to transform us. Isn't that one of the greatest challenges in life—to become the person God wants us to be? That's where true fulfillment is found, and it's the pursuit of a lifetime.

For me, a healthy view of God's dream and of becoming His master-piece begins by avoiding comparison—in fact, carefully defining who I'm not. I can certainly learn by observing the talents and failures of others, but God didn't call me to be a carbon copy of them. He created me to be an original edition. If I spend my time comparing my status to others and checking where I am on the acceptability scale, my focus is entirely on me, not on God and His purposes. Most of the time, comparison produces either pride (if I think I'm doing better than others) or dis-couragement (if I'm not doing as well). In other words, comparison kills. The only measuring stick I need is Christ's pure devotion to the Father's will. Men and women whom God is using in big ways inspire me, but I always have to realize that God has a tailor-made curriculum and plan designed just for me. In a beautiful psalm of confession and trust, David wrote,

> The Lord says, "I will guide you along the best pathway for your
>   life.
> I will advise you and watch over you.
> Do not be like a senseless horse or mule
> that needs a bit and bridle to keep it under control"
> (Psalm 32:8,9, NLT).

Some of us don't pursue God's dream because we're deeply disap-pointed that He hasn't already come through like we hoped He would. When my dad died, it sure seemed like the end of a dream, but God had other plans. In His wisdom and grace, God used that tragedy as an important thread in the tapestry He was weaving for my life. Today, I keep a picture of my father in my teaching notebook to remind me of his example and inspire me to be the man God wants me to be. As we'll see in many stories in this book, our kind and creative God will use anything—absolutely anything—to get our attention, teach us rich lessons, and put us in a place where He can use us in magnificent ways. One of the joys of my life is that God regularly gives me connections with kids of single parents. I understand them because I've been there, and they instinctively know that I "get" them. In the hands of God, the greatest loss of my life has become a source of my greatest usefulness—to touch the lives of single parents and their children. I wouldn't have chosen that painful path, but God turned tragedy into compassion, love, and powerful words of hope for these dear people. I have no doubt that I wouldn't have the impact God is giving me today if I hadn't suffered the loss of my dad. Through the pain, I had to dig deep to trust in God as my Heavenly Father, experience His love, listen to His direction, and become His partner in the family business of changing lives.

Of course, learning life's richest lessons is a tough curriculum, and like many students, I struggled with the assignments. When I was nineteen and in college, I was furious with God. I accused Him of letting my dad die because He didn't care. I told Him He was uncaring and unjust, and I'd had enough. At a critical moment, God sent a man who had known my father—Coach Forrest Arnold. Coach Arnold didn't know that I was thinking about bailing out on God and His dream for my life. He simply put his hand on my shoulder, looked into my eyes, and said: "Doug, your father would be very proud of you. As long as you're in school here, I consider you to be my own son." My heart melted. That's what I longed to hear, and God sent a friend of my dad's to give me that message. Coach Arnold kept me from aborting the dream. At that moment, I began to see that God had been at work—mysteriously and silently behind the scenes—to make me the person He wanted me to be. I began to trust God with my past and my future. It made sense to trust God with my future. Not only does He live outside of time, but He is in the future and already knows what's going to happen for all eternity. In fact, I now believe that God often uses our deepest wounds and biggest failures to shape our lives and propel us to fulfill His dreams for us.

To be sure, a walk of faith protects us from some of life's difficulties, but certainly not all of them. Some Christians believe God owes them blessings and peace because they've gone to church regularly, quit cussing, given generously, or done some other good deed. We need to remember that the ultimately faithful One, Jesus, wasn't exempt from suffering. In fact, He was "a man of sorrows and acquainted with grief" *because* He was faithful to the Father to go to the cross (Isaiah 53:3, KJV).

God sometimes airlifts us out of the storms of life, but far more often, He walks with us through them. He promises blessings, but financial wealth and physical health aren't the only ways He blesses. Far more important, He blesses us with a sense of His nearness and strength as we endure times of difficulty and darkness. We need to have a richer, deeper, more robust view of the character of God. The example of faithful men and women in Scripture and in history shows us that true greatness is often shaped in the crucible of suffering and heartache. God's classroom is full of tests, often severe tests. When we encounter them, we don't need to wonder if He's left us. He's right beside us, cheering us on and offering an arm to cling to.

Two Sauls

Some people are afraid they've missed out on God's dream because they've failed so badly in the past. Their memories are haunted by family conflict, abuse, abandonment, sexual sins, divorce, addictions, or other painful experiences. The good news is that God isn't limited by our past. He always has a dream for our future—if we'll take His hand and follow Him. The Bible tells stories of two men named Saul. One started well, but missed God's dream; the other began poorly, but later found and followed it.

To understand the role of the first Saul, let's start a few centuries before he appeared on the scene. The nation of Israel had a magnificent heritage. Around campfires and kitchen tables, they reminded each other of stories of faith. God called Abraham, and He promised the old man a son and a land. Eventually, God miraculously gave Abraham and Sarah the son they longed for. A couple of generations later, God rescued the family from famine and death when one of their own was betrayed and sold into slavery in Egypt, only to rise to become the prime minister of that nation who administered its food supply so people didn't starve during a famine. The people of God multiplied when they lived in Egypt, but they became slaves. Centuries later, God sent Moses to confront Egypt's stubborn Pharaoh and lead the people to freedom and the land of Promise. There, the people planted gardens and vineyards, and they tended livestock, but they had a continual war against their enemies. Finally, they'd had enough of God ruling over them. They cried out for a king, and reluctantly, God granted their wish. He sent His servant Samuel to anoint as king the tallest, most handsome man in the land—Saul.

At first, the new king led his people to great victories. But he hid a tragic flaw—he was, as Samuel put it, "small in [his] own eyes" (1 Samuel 15:17). His insecurity caused him to doubt God and God's purpose for him. Instead of basking in God's love and purpose and living to honor Him, Saul "set up a monument in his own honor" (1 Samuel 15:12).

God sent him to wipe out a brutal nation, the Amalekites. God instructed Saul not to wage war for profit and keep the spoils of battle, but to be an arm of God's judgment and wipe out every living thing. Saul wanted a victory—not to honor God, but to pad his résumé. He allowed his soldiers to keep the best livestock, and he brought Agag the Amalekite king to his camp. To Saul, the insecure king, all these actions made perfect sense. He could offer a huge sacrifice to God and kill the foreign king to look good in front of all his people. But there was a big problem—he had disobeyed God's clear directives. When Samuel confronted him, Saul made excuses and blamed his soldiers, but the prophet would hear none of it. He told Saul:

> *Does the LORD delight in burnt offerings and sacrifices*
> *as much as in obeying the voice of the LORD?*
> *To obey is better than sacrifice,*
> *and to heed is better than the fat of rams.*
> *For rebellion is like the sin of divination,*
> *and arrogance like the evil of idolatry.*
> *Because you have rejected the word of the LORD,*
> *he has rejected you as king (1 Samuel 15:22,23).*

At that point, God sent Samuel to anoint another man, David, to be the king of His people. The story of Saul is a sad tale. He had everything going for him. He was tall, dark and handsome; he was wealthy; and he had all the power as the nation's king. But his self-perception betrayed him. He was "small in [his] own eyes," so he spent his life trying to win approval from others. Eventually, he fell on his sword and ended his life.

The second Saul is a mirror image of the first one. After Jesus died, rose from the dead, and ascended to heaven, His ragtag group of followers waited in Jerusalem. The Holy Spirit fell on them at Pentecost, and they spoke boldly about the saving grace of Christ to everyone they met. At every point, they faced fierce opposition from the same religious leaders who had stood in Jesus' way. The priests and Pharisees arrested Peter and John, and soon they drew blood by stoning Philip, the first martyr for the cause. As the men who wanted to stone Stephen took off their cloaks to join in the execution, they laid them at the feet of Saul of Tarsus. But Saul wasn't content to remain a passive bystander. He was a rising star in the Jewish community, trained by Gamaliel, one of the foremost rabbis of the day. To squash the movement before it could spread very far, Saul went from city to city to arrest Christians, throw them in jail, and execute them. Stephen may have been the first martyr of the Christian church, but Saul was the first terrorist against it.

When Saul was traveling to Damascus to capture and kill believers, Jesus appeared to him, blinding him with grace and truth. When Saul entered the city, he gave a very different message than the one Jewish leaders expected to hear. He told them that Jesus was, indeed, the long-awaited Messiah, the Lamb of God who takes away the sins of the world. From that time, Saul became God's man to take the gospel to the Gentiles across the Roman Empire, and he began using his Roman name, Paul. Did Paul find and follow God's dream for him? Perhaps as much as any human being who ever lived. He traveled thousands of miles to tell people about Jesus. In his wake, churches sprang up all across the empire, and countless people trusted in Christ. Why was Paul so passionate and tenacious? He filled his letters with specific references to how Christ had gripped his heart by His grace. In his first letter to the Corinthians, he told them that he had been "bought at a price" of Christ's blood (1 Corinthians 6:20, 7:23). In his second letter to them, he explained his motivation: "For Christ's love compels us, because we are convinced that one died for all, and therefore all died. And he died for all, that those who live should no longer live for themselves but for him who died for them and was raised again" (2 Corinthians 5:14,15). And as he was on his way back to Jerusalem after a grueling trip to visit the churches, he told the leaders of the church in Ephesus, "And now, compelled by the Spirit, I am going to Jerusalem, not knowing what will happen to me there. I only know that in every city the Holy Spirit warns me that prison and hardships are facing me. However, I consider my life worth nothing to me; my only aim is to finish the race and complete the task the Lord Jesus has given me—the task of testifying to the good news of God's grace" (Acts 20:22–24).

For Paul, living in 3D wasn't always sweet and smooth. He enjoyed the richest blessings in his walk with God and in wonderful relationships with those who found Christ as he spoke to them, but he also endured open hostility from a host of opponents. He was beaten, flogged, imprisoned, stoned, shipwrecked, and forgotten. Still, he knew he was in the center of God's dream for his life. As he approached the end, he wrote to Timothy, "For I am already being poured out like a drink offering, and the time for my departure is near. I have fought the good fight, I have finished the race, I have kept the faith. Now there is in store for me the crown of righteousness, which the Lord, the righteous Judge, will award to me on that day—and not only to me, but also to all who have longed for his appearing" (2 Timothy 4:6–8).

Every day after he met Christ on the road to Damascus, Paul kept himself in the middle of God's dream for his life, and at the end as he looked back, he could say, "It's almost over, and it's been a great ride." The blessings of living in 3D don't end when we die. As Paul mentioned, the most incredible blessings begin when we take our last breath. Living in the center of God's purpose stores up a crown Christ will put on our heads when we see Him face to face.

Sadly, I know a lot of people like the Saul of the Old Testament. They have incredible advantages of health, wealth, technology, and opportunity, but they sit around complaining that they need more before they're willing to take a step to honor God. They go to church, but they're just checking it off their list of things "good people" do. There's no passion, delight, joy, or gratitude that drives them to love God with all their hearts and serve Him in any way they can.

But thankfully, I know plenty of wonderful people like Saul in the New Testament. If you ask about their stories, they all have checkered pasts. Some were thieves, some were addicts, some had been devastated by abuse, some had sexual hang-ups, some were bitter and selfish, and some endured broken relationships and shattered trust. But they all had a life-changing encounter with Jesus—their own Damascus Road experience—which radically changed them forever. No matter what happened to them in the past, and no matter what sins they committed, they simply can't get over the astounding fact that Jesus Christ loves them and paid the price to rescue them from sin, meaninglessness, and hell. And their hearts sing for joy.

Putting on Our Glasses

Significant parts of God's dream for us are universal. They're in the owner's manual for every believer. God has transferred all believers from the kingdom of darkness into the kingdom of light. Our task each day is to love God with our whole heart, listen to the Spirit, walk with integrity, and touch the lives of others with compassion. This is God's dream for Billy Graham, and it's His dream for a Christian who works at the car wash; the bank executive and the oil field worker; Wall Street, Main Street, and the pastures; those who are the face of the faith in our communities and those few people ever notice. In his excellent book, *The Call*, Os Guinness defines *calling* this way: *"the truth that God calls us to himself so decisively that everything we are, everything we do, and everything we have is invested with a special devotion and dynamism lived out as a response to his summons and service."*[5] That's the general dream for all believers, but as we saw in Paul's letter to the Ephesians, God has a specific dream for each individual believer.

How do we find our specific dream? We need to put on our spiritual glasses so we can see more clearly. God uses a combination of factors to show us what He wants us to do. These factors are desire, talent, and opportunity. Dreaming in 3D always involves the interplay of those three things.

Desire

Few of us last long in any endeavor that fails to capture our hearts. When we watch people play professional sports, we sometimes hear them say, "I love this game so much that I'd pay them to let me play!" In the same spirit, some of us go to work each day with a heart of eager anticipation. We love what we do, and we've become good at it. Desire, though, may come from the opposite direction. A few years ago, Bill Hybels, pastor of Willow Creek Community Church near Chicago, said that God's dream is often the product of "holy discontent." We notice that a need isn't being met, and something stirs in our hearts. We want to do whatever it takes to meet that need. Hybels reminded his readers of the great philosopher, Popeye. When confronted with a problem that cried out for attention, Popeye flexed his muscles and exclaimed, "That's all I can stands, and I can't stands it no more!" He then downed a can of spinach and launched into the task.[6]

Our hearts may be gripped by a need at work, in church, at home, in the community, or overseas. Our hearts may break when we see the plight of unwed mothers, the homeless, addicts, earthquake victims, prisoners, sex slaves, victims of other kinds of abuse, or people who haven't heard the gospel. In response, we can't sit by and watch. We feel compelled to do something. We may weave our passion to help into our normal schedule, or we may use time after work, on weekends, or in the summer to dive in. We aren't constrained by the walls of our churches. The Good Samaritan didn't find the beaten man between the pews; he found him on the side of the road, and he cared for him in every way.

What are things that capture your heart? What needs are going unmet that you feel anxious about? What heartaches in others' lives keep you up at night? When you watch the news, what brings a tear to your eye? Those may be signs God is uncovering a desire that is connected to His dream for you.

Talent

When we look at great paintings, we notice that different artists use different techniques to paint. In the same way, God has given each of us different talents and abilities to use in fulfilling His dream for us. The list is almost endless. The Scriptures have four lists of spiritual gifts, but they list different sets of abilities (Romans 12:3–8, 1 Corinthians 12:7–11, Ephesians 4:11–13, and 1 Peter 4:10,11). This means that

If several trusted people tell you the same thing—positive or negative—take it to heart.

either the writers needed an editor or the list is bigger than these four lists. I believe the talents God gives us are incredibly varied and almost limitless. We discover them in two ways: trial and error, and feedback. We may not know what we do well, so we dive in to counsel a troubled friend, lead a small group, take care of a neighbor's kids, administrate a project at work, care for an elderly person, or a hundred other things. Gradually (or not so gradually) we realize, "Hey, that went pretty well, and I really enjoyed it. I could sense God's presence as I did it." That's a sign we're in our sweet spot. Honest feedback from others confirms our perceptions, or in some cases, gives us needed encouragement to keep going. Occasionally, people lack self-perception so much that they think they're doing great but get negative feedback from others. If this happens to you, ask others to give you an objective analysis of what you're doing. If several trusted people tell you the same thing—positive or negative—take it to heart. The focus, though, isn't on our gifts; it's on God. Os Guinness notes, *"God normally calls us along the line of our giftedness, but the purpose of giftedness is stewardship and service, not selfishness."*[7]

Opportunity

Investing our talents in all kinds of projects implies that we have ample opportunities to try them out. In most families, businesses, and churches, people are more than happy for you to volunteer for a role. If you experience fulfillment and success, everybody wins. If you don't, try something else. Some of us are convinced that we have great talent in an area, but no opportunity surfaces. It's like the lady who is sure she has the gift of singing, but no one around her has the gift of listening to her. To be sure, some roles require a little more effort to find opportunities, but don't expect them to knock on your door and beg. If you have the desire and you think you have talent in an area, ask for an open door of opportunity.

Alignment

When a gifted artist wants to produce a beautiful sculpture, he doesn't just throw the clay onto the table and hope it works out. When a painter wants to create a masterpiece, she doesn't sling colors on the canvas and hope everything will look good. Artists—especially the most skilled ones—invest time and attention in aligning every feature of their work so that it goes well. In the same way, we need to devote energy and resources in organizing our lives to fulfill the dream God gives us.

In my life, when I sensed God was leading me to vocational Christian ministry, I considered where I might go to college, whom I would date and marry, my choice of friends, and the types of experiences that would equip me. I needed to align my ambitions, talents, and resources with God's dream. Today, years later, I still do the same thing. I'm most fulfilled as I align my daily decisions with God's calling, purpose, and dream for my life. As I have made major decisions that involved ministry and career changes, I have kept a scorecard that reads:

God's man: Does the role fit me?
God's time: Does the timing fit my family and my sense of direction?
God's place: Is God leading me to that particular place with those people?

If those criteria don't line up, I know which choice won't lead me to a 3D dream.

Here's another example: An attorney had been an alcoholic for thirty years, and he had committed adultery with a woman in his office. He came close to losing everything he valued, but like the Prodigal Son in Jesus' story, he "came to his senses" (Luke 15:17). The attorney met Christ, joined a recovery group, and went through months of counseling with his wife to begin to rebuild trust. Over the course of several years, he uncovered God's dream for him. He desired to help alcoholics find Christ and turn their lives around, and he became a leader in a recovery ministry at his church. By his own admission, he had been "a self-absorbed fool" when he was addicted. But today, he is known for his humility and generosity. As desire, talent, and opportunity have become clear, he has aligned his time and money for a more powerful impact on his clients, co-workers, friends, and dozens of people in his community.

People sometimes make a category mistake and rank a pastor's dream above a plumber's dream, but there is no sacred/secular dichotomy, no higher or lower order of dreams, no 3D or rabbit ears. God's dreams for each of us are equal in His sight. When Martin Luther launched the Protestant Reformation in the early sixteenth century, he focused on the power of grace to change lives, but he also revolutionized our understanding of the meaning of work. For centuries, the Church had taught that being a pastor, monk, or nun was valuable to God, but being a farmer, carpenter, or mother had little, if any, meaning. Luther disagreed. He wrote:

> *The works of monks and priests, however holy and arduous they may be, do not differ one whit in the sight of God from the works of the rustic laborer in the field or the woman going about her household tasks, but... all works are measured before God by faith alone. . . . Indeed, the menial housework of a manservant or maidservant is often more acceptable to God than all the fasting and other works of a monk or priest, because the monk or priest lacks faith.[8]*

In fact, Luther turned the false teaching upside down because he taught we are all priests who love and serve God in our vocations. The question every church must answer is not, "Is the pastor fulfilling God's dream?" but, "Are all the people in the church finding and fulfilling God's dream?"

Never Too Late

One of the most powerful and consistent principles in the Bible is that it's never too late to get in on God's dream. Over and over again, we find men and women who blew it—big time—but God graciously restored them and used them. God isn't looking for perfect people. He's looking for repentant, responsive people. We could look at many different examples in the Bible, but Peter stands out. He was the chief spokesman among the twelve disciples who walked with Jesus. As Jesus ate His last meal with them before His death, He told them that He would suffer and die. Peter insisted, "Lord, I am ready to go with you to prison and to death" (Luke 22:33). But, of course, a few hours later as he warmed himself next to a fire, he denied that he even knew Jesus. His failure crushed him. As the rooster crowed, he "went outside and wept bitterly" (Luke 22:52). A few hours later, Jesus was killed cruelly. In the days that followed, Peter concluded that he was washed up as a disciple, but Jesus had other plans. When Peter and some others went fishing, probably because they had given up on the cause, Jesus appeared on the shore and cooked them some fish. The smell of a charcoal fire that morning undoubtedly reminded Peter of his worst failure, when he denied Jesus by another fire days before. But Jesus gently restored him. Peter had denied Jesus three times, so Jesus asked him three times, "do you love me?" (John 21:15–17). The fisherman received assurance of Jesus' forgiveness, and he soon became the mouthpiece of the Church, leading thousands to faith on its first day of existence (Acts 2:41).

If it wasn't too late for Peter—or Abraham or Jacob or Rahab or Samson or David or Josiah or many others in the Scriptures—it's not too late for us. If we'll let Him, God will use our greatest failures to soften our hearts and fill us with compassion for others who similarly suffer or sin. The Son of God is fully aware of our flaws and our capacity to fail, but He still says, "I have a dream for you." That gives me a world of hope.

Ultimately, God's dream isn't an easy life, but a rich and meaningful one. If we're willing to take His hand, it's the ride of a lifetime. Theologian J. I. Packer gives us hope and encouragement about our most painful experiences:

> *This is what all the work of grace aims at—an even deeper knowledge of God, and an ever closer fellowship with Him. Grace is God drawing us sinners closer and closer to Him. How does God in grace prosecute this purpose? Not by shielding us from assault by the world, the flesh, and the devil, nor by protecting us from burdensome and frustrating circumstances, nor yet by shielding us from troubles created by our own temperament and psychology; but rather by exposing us to all these things, so as to overwhelm us with a sense of our own inadequacy, and to drive us to cling to Him more closely. This is the ultimate reason, from our standpoint, why God fills our lives with troubles and perplexities of one sort or another—it is to ensure that we shall learn to hold Him fast.[9]*

"Here's the Church"

We don't find and follow God's dream in a vacuum. We need one another to point us, prod us, and protect us. We are all more effective and fulfilled when others step into our lives to help us uncover our potential and share the wisdom we need when we get stuck. And sometimes, we just need a smile and a hug.

I heard a story about a little girl who had lost her arm in an accident. Her family moved, and she had to go to a new school—a private school at a church. The little girl was anxious about how she might be received. A few kids stared at her empty sleeve, but the teacher welcomed her warmly. Later that morning, the class recited the familiar rhyme,

Here's the church, and here's the steeple,
Open the door and see all the people.

As the class did the hand motions, the teacher looked at the little girl. The boy next to her leaned over and smiled. He put his hand with hers, they did the motions together. All it took was a little love and creativity to make a little girl's dream of being included come true. We have that same opportunity many times each day as we pass by people. If we notice them, we might play a key role in helping them find and follow God's dream.

At the end of each chapter, you'll find some questions. When I read books, I get far more out of them if I take a few minutes to reflect on the principles the author presents. These questions are designed for two purposes: for individual reflection and, if you use this book in a group, to stimulate discussion. The goal isn't to rush through them to fill in the blanks. Take your time, pray, and ask the Lord to help you uncover His dream for you, your family, and your friends.

What's Your Take?

1. Who are some people you know (maybe only one) who lives a life of purpose and meaning? What about their lives is most attractive to you?

2. Read Ephesians 2:10. How does it encourage you to think that you are God's masterpiece? What difference would it (or does it) make to see yourself that way?

3. What are some reasons people miss God's dream? How does missing it affect them spiritually, emotionally, relationally, and physically?

4. How would you describe the differences between the two Sauls? Which one best represents your life today? Explain your answer.

5. Describe how people uncover their dream by paying attention to desire, talents, and opportunities. Where are you in this process?

6. On a scale of 0 (not clear at all) to 10 (crystal clear), how clear is God's dream for you? Explain your answer.

7. How does it encourage you to think of Peter's example that it's never too late to find and follow your dream?

8. Can you articulate God's dream for your life, or are you still in process of defining and describing it? If it's already clear, state it here. If there are still some pieces of the puzzle that aren't in place yet, take some time to pray, think, and write the answers to these questions:

   Desire: How do you want God to use you? What kind of impact excites you? What are some evidences of "holy discontent" in your life? What needs in others' lives capture your heart?

Talent: What do you do at work, at home, and for the church that "feels right," like God's hand is on you when you do it? What are the abilities others identify and affirm in your life? What are some skills that you want to develop even more?

Opportunity: What are some roles you've already stepped into that are fulfilling and fruitful? What are some roles that are interesting to you? Where have you been asked to take more responsibility?

9. As you've considered these three factors (desire, talent, and opportunity), has your dream gotten any clearer? If not, what are some steps you can take to identify these factors more clearly? Don't be alarmed if it's not clear yet. Finding a 3D dream takes time, experience, feedback, and tenacity. I trust that as you read this book, God will reveal His direction to you.

Prayer of Commitment

Lord Jesus, thank You that it's never too late, and You're more than happy to show me Your dream for my life. Thank You for Your goodness and grace. Lord, I'm open. Show me who You want me to be and what You want me to do. I'm Yours. Amen.

2 The Power of a Dream

Our job is not to climb the ladder of success, but to descend the ladder of servanthood.

—Anonymous

Jason McElwain had been the manager of the varsity basketball team for Athena High School in Rochester, New York, but he longed to play the game. Jason, though, was autistic. The players enjoyed his enthusiasm, and Coach Jim Johnson wanted to encourage the young man. For the last game of the year, he gave Jason a uniform and added him to the team. When the team was well ahead with only four minutes to play, Johnson sent Jason into the game. Later, Jason related, "My first shot was an air ball—by a lot. Then I missed a lay up. As the first shot went in, and then the second shot, as soon as that went in, I just started to catch fire!" Jason sank six three-point shots and a two-pointer, finishing the four minutes of his playing career with twenty points. It was a dream come true, but not just for Jason. After the buzzer sounded, ending the game, Jason's teammates and the crowd carried him off the court. He grinned, "I felt like a celebrity!"

A clear picture of a preferred future galvanizes our desires, streamlines our priorities, and drives us forward when we encounter obstacles.

It was just as much of a joy for Coach Johnson. He remarked, "I've had a lot of thrills in coaching. I've coached a lot of wonderful kids, but I've never experienced such a thrill."

Jason's mother had a longer, deeper view of what happened that night. She told a reporter, "This is the first moment Jason has ever succeeded and could be proud of himself. I look at autism as the Berlin Wall, and he cracked it."[1]

For centuries, the power of a dream hasn't been a secret. King Solomon announced, "Where there is no vision [or dream], the people perish" (Proverbs 29:18, KJV). A clear picture of a preferred future galvanizes our desires, streamlines our priorities, and drives us forward when we encounter obstacles. To find and follow a dream, passion is essential.

The Non-Negotiables

Passion is neutral; it can be positive or negative, depending on the power source. Every day, news accounts are littered with stories of people who were passionate for selfish gain. In sports, politics, business, and every other field of endeavor, selfish people use others as stepping stones to get where they want to go. Some of them appear to be noble and good as they manipulate others to climb the ladder of success. When they are exposed, however, they usually blame someone else for their own tragic flaws. Countless others, though, live numb, passionless lives. Maybe they tried something great earlier and failed, and at some point they simply gave up on ever making a difference. Or maybe they simply don't have enough self-confidence to reach for the stars. But there's another category of people—those who have a beautiful blend of contentment and drive, whose hearts have been melted by seeing others' needs. Their holy discontent drives them to attempt great things—not for self-glory, but for others. Those who walk with Christ often exhibit two powerful traits that prompt and purify passion: they are supernaturally *anointed* by God to fulfill a kingdom purpose, and in the process, they exemplify Christ's *humility*.

GREAT

There are plenty of strange ideas about the concept of anointing. Let me clarify things: An anointing is supernatural assistance to fulfill your dreams. It is "the God factor," the insertion of heaven's resources and power into a person's life to ful-fill his or her appointed purpose. To be a clear channel of the Spirit's work through us, we must continually clean out the selfishness, defensiveness, resentment, and entitlement that are

> **The anointing, however, can only take us as far as our character will let us go.**

endemic to the human condition. How do we address those poisonous heart issues? By focusing on the humility of Christ and letting His attitude of being a servant permeate our thoughts, words, and actions. Both of these elements—God's anointing and our humility—provide enormous power to find and fulfill God's dream in our lives. The anointing, however, can only take us as far as our character will let us go. Saul was anointed by God, but his disobedience disqualified him. A humble heart longs for God's will, God's ways, and God's timing.

One of the rarest traits among *Homo sapiens* is humility, but many people misunderstand what it is. It is not thinking less of yourself, but thinking of yourself less. C. S. Lewis said that a humble person, "will not be thinking about himself at all."[2] We aren't humble when we are self-critical and wallow in shame. That's just as self-absorbed as arrogant pride, but it's the flip side of it. No, true humility is being consumed by Someone and something greater than ourselves. It's letting the grace of God solve our innate problem of radical insecurity so that we don't have to think about ourselves all day, every day. The grace of God is the foundation of a humble heart. When we realize that we are totally forgiven and fully accepted by the almighty God of the universe—not because we've earned it, but because it's a free gift—we can breath a deep sigh of relief, soak in the joy of being loved, and then turn our eyes outward to the needs of others.

In his second letter to the Corinthians, Paul explained the incredible grace of God and His purposes for us. Then, he wrote about our motivation: "Therefore we also have as our ambition, whether at home or absent, to be pleasing to Him" (2 Corinthians 5:9, NASB). At first, this seems like a very odd thing for the apostle to say. We usually think of ambition as a sin, but it is noble or sinful depending on its object. When the grace and love of Christ flood our hearts, and we realize we're more valuable to Him than the stars in the sky, our motivations are purified and we want—more than anything in the world—to make Him smile. But Paul knew very well that the default mode of the human heart is away from this kind of attitude. He warned the Corinthians, "But I am afraid that just as Eve was deceived by the serpent's cunning, your minds may somehow be led astray from your sincere and pure devotion to Christ" (2 Corinthians 11:3). This is another astounding statement from Paul. He wasn't afraid of much, was he? He went to city after city expecting to be ridiculed, stoned, whipped, imprisoned, and castigated. He was one of the most courageous people the world has ever known. But here, he says he's afraid. Of what? He was afraid that the Corinthians' minds would be deceived and they'd value worthless things instead of Christ. I'm sure he'd have the same fear for us today.

One of my favorite moments in movies is in *Chariots of Fire*. The great Scottish runner, Eric Liddell, had refused to run a qualifying sprint at the 1924 Olympics in Paris because it had been scheduled on the Sabbath, and he believed running on the Lord's Day would dishonor God. He dropped out of a race he was picked to win, but another runner gave him a slot in the 400-meter race. Before that race began, American runner Jackson Scholz handed Liddell a piece of paper with an inscription from 1 Samuel 2:30: "It says in the Good Book, 'He that honors me, I will honor.' Good luck." Clutching the paper in his hand, Liddell ran the race and won—for the glory of God.

The Scriptures contain many passages about God's desire for us to have humble hearts. Humility, though, is so counterintuitive that we can't develop it on our own. It requires the deep work of the Spirit of God to produce this rare quality in us, but we can be sure it's what God wants. In one of my favorite passages about God's intentions for us, the prophet Micah tells the people:

> *He has shown you, O mortal, what is good.*
> *And what does the LORD require of you?*
> *To act justly and to love mercy*
> *and to walk humbly with your God (Micah 6:8).*

Humility points us to God's provisions of grace and strength. When we think that all depends on us, the weight of the world is on us, and we feel driven, act defensively, and get discouraged. But when we recognize Christ's rightful place in the center of our lives, and we trust Him to accomplish His will in and through us, we can relax. We still work hard, but in a spirit of partnership with God, neither isolated from Him nor demanding that He jump through our hoops and meet our expectations. Humility is a source of great joy, a wealth of love, and a deep well of true compassion for others. A humble heart unleashes the grace and power of God. James said, "God opposes the proud, but gives grace to the humble" (James 4:6, ESV). I sure want to be on the right side of that equation.

When I arrived at my first pastorate, the church was severely hurting and deeply divided. I followed a trio of tragedies, especially in the way the pastors preceding me left the church. One left because of interpersonal conflict, another because of sexual indiscretion, and the third because of poor financial management. I was a rookie pastor trying to honor the Lord, and I didn't know what to do. When I arrived, I immediately saw the hurt, anger, and distrust among the people I was supposed to shepherd. At that crucial moment, God overwhelmed me with a spirit of humility and gave me words that healed and built trust. Since then, I've often used those words. When I encounter anger or power struggles, instead of being defensive and trying to control everybody, I say two things: "I don't know" and "Would you help?" These statements show people that I'm not a threat. They build trust and enlist the support of those who have a choice to be enemies or friends.

A God-given dream gives shape and meaning to our lives. It directs our choices, energizes our bodies, and gives us tenacity to keep going when others want to quit. Christians have a decided advantage because we know the end of the story. Our lives are infused with meaning because we serve the Creator of the universe, the Savior of mankind, and the One who says, "Well done!" whenever we do anything for Him.

Our Entitlement Culture

In our society, people value the external. We work hard and pursue success, promotions, money, sex, and power. These things, we've been promised in countless ads, will give us ultimate fulfillment. But this promise is a lie. God has made us so that we can only be temporarily satisfied with self-absorbed pursuits. Augustine rightly observed that only God can fill the hole in our hearts. He wrote, "you have made us for yourself, and our heart is restless until it rests in you."[3] When the circle of our lives is reduced to a dot, we realize that there must be something more to life than acquiring stuff and filling our lives with empty pleasures. After years of acquiring wealth and building his reputation, legendary automaker Lee Iacocca lamented, "Here I am in the twilight years of my life, still wondering what it's all about. I can tell you this.... fame and fortune is for the birds."[4] Self-focused success—even stunning success—thrills us only for a moment. As a character is a Walker Percy novel puts it, "I made straight A's and flunked ordinary living."[5] Not having a God-inspired dream to guide our actions is flunking life. In the last few years, a movement has encouraged people to find and follow a compelling purpose. Rick Warren's *The Purpose Driven Life* has sold over thirty million copies and changed many lives. We can't live on yesterday's insights and last year's meaning. We need to keep pursuing, keep pushing, and keep clarifying the reason we get up each day.

We live in an entitlement culture—not just in government welfare programs, but in the sense that we deserve life to be easy, fun, and exciting. For most of us, "the good life" and "the American dream" aren't just pursuits; they're demands. When we don't get what we want, we whine, pout, and sue people to get it. Charles J. Sykes's perceptive book, *A Nation of Victims*, describes the litigious nature of our culture, in which we are quick to file lawsuits to get what we think we deserve.[6] Our culture is filled with deceptive messages that we deserve an ever-increasing amount of possessions and pleasure, and our demand for these things chokes our values and purposes. Daniel Yankelovich, author of *New Rules*, observes that in the past sixty years, our culture has shifted from self-sacrifice to self-indulgence.[7] The generation that willingly gave their lives to defeat totalitarianism in Germany, Italy, and Japan would hardly recognize us today. No wonder so many of the "Greatest Generation" shake their heads when they see what's going on in our culture.

Turn Down the Volume

I'm afraid that some of us miss God's dream for us, or we misinterpret the dream, because we're so distracted by all the busyness of life. We run from one meeting to another, from our kid's game to a church function, and we have the television, DVD, or music on all the time. Families seldom sit down for meals together, and if they do, they do so in front of the television, with the predictable result that they don't talk to each other (except to argue about the channel). Kids and adults are connected to friends, family, and co-workers at every moment of every day by cell phone, text messaging, email, and Facebook. We are the most plugged-in society in the world, rarely turning off the sights and sounds to come up for air.

The omnipresence of technology has a powerful impact on individuals and their capacity to communicate. It especially has cut short time with our kids. Linda Stone, formerly of Apple and Microsoft, coined the term *continuous partial attention* to describe the constant distractions of e-mail, instant messages, cell phones, and other forms of communication. She reports:

To pay continuous partial attention is to pay partial attention— CONTINUOUSLY. It is motivated by a desire to be a LIVE node on the network. Another way of saying this is that we want to connect and be connected. We want to effectively scan for opportunity and optimize for the best opportunities, activities, and contacts, in any given moment. To be busy, to be connected, is to be alive, to be recognized, and to matter.

We pay continuous partial attention in an effort NOT TO MISS ANYTHING. It is an always-on, anywhere, anytime, any place behavior that involves an artificial sense of constant crisis. We are always in high alert when we pay continuous partial attention. This artificial sense of constant crisis is more typical of continuous partial attention than it is of multi-tasking.[8]

I have to admit that I struggle with this. Like most people today, I use technology to stay connected, but when I'm checking my status on Twitter during a church service—especially when I'm preaching—I'm too plugged-in. As a discipline, I have to carve out times when I disconnect and enjoy undistracted time with my family and the Lord. I call this *the sacredness of silence.*

Another factor that erodes passion is the ever-present and powerful force of advertising. Though advertising certainly isn't the only cause of our discontent, it has a powerful impact on our expectations. The purpose of advertising is to create dissatisfaction, to make us crave more than we have so we'll buy this product or use that service. The real message of ads isn't that the product or service will whiten our teeth, help us run faster, enable us to enjoy the latest technology, or add to our bank balance. No, the real promise of every ad is ultimate fulfillment: we simply can't be truly happy and content without buying a certain products. The problem for serious Christians is that we swim in this water too. Professor Philip Kenneson has observed that it's easy for believers to think that following Christ is only one more consumer choice, to be valued or discarded as it suits us. In his book, *Life on the Vine*, he writes:

> *Living in a culture like ours also encourages Christians to frame their understanding of the faith primarily in terms of self-interest. (What's in it for me? Plenty! Start with eternal life.) Hence, many people are "converted" less out of their sense that they are estranged from God and other people and their desire to be reconciled, but more out of a sense that they're savvy consumers, knowing a good deal when they see one.[9]*

People in churches can become infected with this deadly virus of consumer thinking, but because it's so common, we seldom even realize we're infected. Instead of being overwhelmed with the matchless grace of God and devoting our whole hearts to honor the One who bought us and rescued us, those of us who are infected with the disease of consumerism see the Christian faith as a deal—maybe one we can't pass up. Instead of asking, "Is Christianity true?" we instinctively ask, "Will Christ make me happy?" and "Is Christianity my best option for personal fulfillment?" If the claims of Christ aren't true, then Christianity is a colossal fraud, not a nice and hopeful philosophy that leads to personal gain. But if it's true, our hearts are captured by God's love, and we follow Jesus wherever He leads us—into light and into darkness, in good times and bad. The hymn writer Isaac Watts understood that Jesus has a categorical claim on our lives because of God's grace. He wrote:

Love so amazing, so divine,

demands my soul, my life, my all.[10]

Far too often, we focus our attention on the wrong dream—having more and bigger stuff, including more and bigger ministries. But sometimes we're riveted on the right dream, but we're so driven and busy that we lose touch with the Spirit. Even if we're right in the center of God's purpose for us, we need to cultivate quiet so we can listen to the whisper of the Spirit. I believe the power of a dream can't be realized unless we take time to listen to Him.

The Object

The size and intensity of a person's dream isn't as important as its object. A dream can be noble or selfish, inspiring us to touch others' lives or driving us to "get all we can" and "can all we get." If we look around, we find wonderful stories of men and women who weren't content to settle for the status quo. Their hearts were gripped by the needs of others. With a profound sense of drive, they developed a plan and took bold steps of action to meet those needs.

> **The size and intensity of a person's dream isn't as important as its object.**

Blake Mycoskie and his sister were on the reality television show, *The Amazing Race*, and part of their worldwide adventure took them to Argentina. He was fascinated by Argentine culture, and he returned there for a vacation in 2006. As he walked the streets, he saw that many children lacked shoes. He decided to sell his online driver-education company to raise the capital to start a shoe company. This shoe company had a novel business model: to give away a pair of shoes to needy children for every pair sold. Blake later recalled, "I was sitting on a farm pondering life, and it occurred to me, 'I'm going to start a shoe company, and for every pair that we sell, I'll give a pair to someone who needs them.'"[11] His company, TOMS Shoes, gives away shoes all over the world. To capture people's attention, the company promotes an annual event, "One Day Without Shoes." In a recent year, over 250,000 people went barefoot for a day to make others aware of children who need shoes.

In the 1950s, American culture was very different than it is today. Segregation was the law and custom of the land, and little had been accomplished for African Americans since the end of the Civil War. In Montgomery, Alabama, in December 1955, one woman had enough. A bus driver told Rosa Parks to sit in the back of the bus where other people of color sat, but she refused. Her courageous defiance ignited passions, and fifty thousand people—black and white—boycotted the city's bus system for over a year. Dr. Martin Luther King Jr., a young, charismatic Atlanta preacher, came to offer his support. The brilliantly organized campaign to force the Southern city to reform Jim Crow laws was the tinder box that caught fire, enflaming a nonviolent movement to finish what Radical Reconstruction had begun nearly a century before. It all began because one woman had the guts to say no to discrimination and stand up for justice. Dr. King later wrote, "The ultimate measure of a man is not where he stands in moments of comfort and convenience but where he stands at times of challenge and controversy."[12]

There are countless examples of people whose dream to make a difference in others' lives began with a spark of discontent. Some have started companies or non-profit organizations, but others have simply walked across the street to help someone in need. A few have achieved

celebrity status, but most remain unknown and unheralded. Nc
ever heard of Todd Beamer, but on the morning of September 11, 2001,
on United Flight 93, he and some other passengers realized they were
the last hope of everyone on board. After reciting the Lord's Prayer and
calling his wife to say goodbye, he said, "Let's roll!" and confronted the
hijackers. Undoubtedly, he never thought of acquiring fame that day. He
only wanted to do the right thing at the right time, no matter what the
cost—which is the essence of integrity and courage.

I believe dreams aren't optional. They are part of the divine spark in
every human heart. Especially for Christians, who have an intimate connection with God's love and purposes, the spark bursts into flame when
we see the desperate needs of people, engage our talent, and anticipate in
our hearts what it will mean to others for the need to be met.

Pruned

In the last hundred years or so, most people have moved away from
farms to towns and cities. Today, farming is mechanized and efficient,
so the few farmers remaining on the land raise plenty for the rest of us.
Now, however, most of us don't have any connection to the cycles of
plowing, planting, and harvesting. We are poorer for it. We go to the
grocery store and buy cleaned and packaged vegetables and meat in neat
cellophane-wrapped containers, and we find row after row of canned,
boxed, and bottled goods. Most of us never get our hands dirty. Un-
consciously, I'm afraid that many of us expect the rest of life to work
in this convenient, sanitized way, but it doesn't. Quite often, God takes
our dreams through a cycle much like the natural progression of farming. Before Jesus was arrested and went to the cross, He spent His last
hours with His closest followers. There in the Garden, He shared crucial

information they'd need to remember when times got tough. John re-corded this conversation in detail, and in the middle of his account, he relates Jesus' explanation of spiritual life as a vineyard. Every person hearing it that night and countless generations since have known exactly what Jesus meant. He told His disciples:

> *I am the true vine, and my Father is the gardener. He cuts off every branch in me that bears no fruit, while every branch that does bear fruit he prunes so that it will be even more fruitful. You are already clean because of the word I have spoken to you. Remain in me, as I also remain in you. No branch can bear fruit by itself; it must remain in the vine. Neither can you bear fruit unless you remain in me.*
> *I am the vine; you are the branches. If you remain in me and I in you, you will bear much fruit; apart from me you can do nothing (John 15:1–5).*

Since dreams are an integral part of spiritual life—inherent in God's purposes for all of us—this passage applies to the cycle of growth in our deepest desires. For the owner of a vineyard, pruning is essential for a good harvest each year. From a distance, unregulated growth may look healthy and green, but it results in a lot of wasted energy and few grapes. Each year, the gardener cuts back the vines almost to the ground. The cuts look drastic and harsh, and for the entire winter, those who have never seen a vineyard may think the gardener has made a horrible mistake. But when spring comes and the vine begins growing again, the new growth produces a bumper harvest of grapes. It's the nature of the harvest—in a vineyard and in our spiritual lives.

What does pruning look like for someone's dream? Quite often, it involves failure, criticism, and correction. I've talked to many people who share the same pattern in their stories: God gave them a wonderful dream to touch people's lives, but after an initial burst of progress, things went south. In fact, most of them say they experienced such huge setbacks that they thought their dream was over. After a time, though, God resurrected the dream, now perhaps with purer motives or greater resources or a fresh direction, and the people saw God work more magnificently than they ever dreamed.

The power of a dream isn't static. Even with the best of intentions and plenty of resources, our wise and sovereign God often diverts our path from the mountaintop to the valley. We can't always assume that we've had wrong motives (though they can always be deepened and sharpened), and we can't assume that God has suddenly said no to our dream. He may be saying, "Yes, but not this way, not at this time, and not with that person." We shouldn't assume that pruning is judgment—some kind of rebuke because we've gotten off track. Quite the opposite! A gardener prunes his valuable plants, ones that he treasures and has the greatest hopes for. If God is pruning you, it's a sign of His confidence in you. He's preparing you, your heart, and your resources for the next stage of growth and production.

As God works on our hearts in times of pruning, He may reveal elements of darkness—selfish motives, demands, unrealistic expectations, etc.—we've never noticed before. Throughout our lives, He puts us in situations that test us and strengthen our desire to live with integrity. Billy Graham famously said, "Integrity is the glue that holds our way of life together. We must consistently strive to keep our integrity intact. When wealth is lost, nothing is lost; when health is lost, something is lost; when character is lost, *all* is lost."[13] Integrity is defined more by people's actions than their words. They don't just talk about doing the right thing in difficult circumstances; they do it, even if no one even notices. Being people of integrity doesn't mean we're perfect. Instead, it means we're honest about our failures, we accept responsibility for them, and we do whatever it takes to make them right. People of integrity don't settle for speaking *mottos*; they become *models* of grace, courage, and truth for those around them.

Full Access *Alignment*

As God works deeply in us to align our hearts with His, amazing things happen. God is waiting for us to say, "Not my will but thine." When we say it and mean it, the power of the Spirit flows in us and through us to accomplish the purposes He has put on our hearts. The prophet Hanani told King Asa, "For the eyes of the LORD range throughout the earth to strengthen those whose hearts are fully committed to him." (2 Chronicles 16:9).

In the same way, Dwight L. Moody, one of the great pastors in the history of Chicago and our country, was a man who was gripped with God's calling on his life. He often told people, "It remains to be seen what God will do with a man who gives himself up wholly to him." He always quickly completed the thought by saying, "Well, I will be that man."

> Of course, being in alignment with the Spirit doesn't guarantee smooth sailing.

In a private conversation with the noted pastor and theologian, R. A. Torrey, Moody remarked, "Torrey, if I believed that God wanted me to jump out of that window, I would jump."

Torrey later reflected, "I believe he would. If he thought God wanted him to do anything, he would do it. He belonged wholly, unreservedly, unqualifiedly, entirely, to God."[14]

Of course, being in alignment with the Spirit doesn't guarantee smooth sailing. We only need to look at the life of Jesus to understand this principle. No one has ever been in the center of the Father's will as much as Jesus. He enjoyed times of great acclaim, but He was often misunderstood and eventually killed for His loyalty and obedience to the Father. Our goal is to stand before God one day and hear the words, "Well done, good and faithful servant! You have been faithful with a few things; I will put you in charge of many things. Come and share your master's happiness!" (Matthew 25:21). Ultimately, God holds the measuring stick, and He determines the value of our lives. When Jesus left the earth, even some of the few He left behind doubted Him. By any standard, His life and work didn't appear to be a glowing success, but it was the beginning of a revolution that swept the world.

Some well-intentioned Christians get confused about who is doing the work to fulfill their dreams. They assume that if they do anything at all, they're hindering the Spirit's work. I've heard people say things like, "If it can be explained by any human action, God's not in it." I don't agree. God has chosen to use people like us to accomplish His purposes. We trust Him for wisdom and strength, and we take action to follow His leading. Walking in the Spirit's power isn't either Him *or* us; but a partnership of Him *and* us. We need to avoid the ditches on either side of the road—the ditch of grinding self-effort on one side and magical thinking that God will do it all on the other side. The Spirit's power is active when we listen to His voice, trust Him to guide and use us, and then step out in faith. The Bible says, "The steps of a good man are ordered by the LORD" (Psalm 37:23), but you still have to walk.

One of the most painful things I see in the lives of believers is joyless obedience. They feel oppressed by a smothering sense of guilt, and they live by a litany of *should*s. They've forgotten (or perhaps they've never known) that "the joy of the Lord is [our] strength" (Nehemiah 8:10). Certainly, there are times of difficulty and demands in fulfilling any dream. Between the time a dream is conceived and the time it is achieved, there's a lot of blood, sweat, and tears, but the journey of walking hand in hand with the One who loves us and calls us to be partners in the greatest adventure of life should have an abundance of joys, thrills, and laughs. Don't settle for anything less.

In our experience of God's anointing and our pursuit of humility, we desperately need mentors and friends to walk with us. These roles are different. Mentors are wise, trusted leaders who speak the truth and prod us to go where we've never gone before, but friends are cheerleaders who love us and believe in us no matter what. We need both.

The unfolding of God's dream in our lives contains both certainty and mystery. The Spirit confirms our gifts and opens doors to opportunity, and He uses the feedback of mature believers to confirm or correct our thinking. But at a deep level, God's impartation of a dream is a wondrous, inexplicable thing. Oswald Chambers observed:

If you can tell where you got the call of God and all about it, I question whether you have ever had a call. The call of God does not come like that, it is much more supernatural. The realization of it in a man's life may come with a sudden thunder-clap or with a gradual dawning, but in whatever way it comes, it comes with the undercurrent of the supernatural, something that cannot be put into words.[15]

Mary's Dream

Few people exemplify the power—and the complexity—of a dream as well as Mary, the mother of Jesus. God chose a young girl with a simple, strong faith to bear the Son of God. She was anointed. An angel appeared to her to explain God's divine purpose for her life. And she was humble. She didn't resist the angel's message. She only asked the logical question, "How will this be, since I am a virgin?" (Luke 1:34). When she heard the answer, she took on an incredibly difficult role—far more painful emotionally than physically. From that moment, she endured some of the most difficult pruning anyone has ever experienced. First, she had to explain things to her naturally bewildered fiancé. As a pregnant, unmarried girl, she suffered whispers and ridicule from people in her community. As Jesus grew up, I'm sure other families realized there was something very different about Mary's Son, and in fact, her other children probably resented Jesus always being right—about everything! When Mary watched Jesus begin His ministry, I can imagine her heart swelling with pride when people trusted Him, but it broke in anguish when they attacked Him so viciously. And then, she was crushed as she watched Him endure torture and death on the cross. Almost all the men who had followed Him for three years ran for their lives, but John, Mary, and a few other women were there to the bitter end. After three days, she saw her Son as the risen, glorified Christ, the Lord of glory. And a few weeks later, she watched Him vanish into a cloud.

Mary's story reminds us that finding and fulfilling God's dream is never clean, simple, or easy. There are obstacles, enemies, and heartaches along the way. Many people simply bail out because God's dream is too hard or it's not rewarding soon enough. But those like Mary—those who are enraptured by God's anointing and humbly submit to His ways—see God do amazing things.

One of the most amazing things about Mary was that she wasn't possessive of her treasured Son. She could have tried to protect Him from harm, but she knew that He was fulfilling the Father's purpose. After my dad died, I grew up and prepared to go off to college. My mother could have said, "Doug, I need you here with me," or "You'll never make it out there without me," but she held me with an open hand. In the many years since then, my mom has said many times, "Doug, I've missed you so much since you left home, but the will of God for your life is much bigger than my desire to keep you around. I'm so proud of you for pursing God with all your heart." I don't know if my mother ever equated her life with Mary, but both of these dear women recognized the incredible value of their God-given dream, and they didn't let any selfish desires destroy it.

For each of us, a God-size dream inspires us to trust God and work hard to fulfill it, but size and numbers aren't always the measure of God's dreams. We are wrong if we think we have to become famous, powerful, or wealthy to be the person God wants us to be. Far from it! Mary and my mother experienced the fulfillment of God's dream when they raised boys with an open hand and helped them become strong young men. Others are called to be the best home school parent and teacher they can be, care for an elderly relative, love a special needs child, gather canned goods for a food pantry, build homes for the unfortunate, raise teenagers to be wise young men and women, or become a beacon of God's light at work. Like Mary and my mom, though, there is a time when God breaks into our consciousness to identify the dream He gives us. He then assures us that He will fulfill it—in His timing, in His way, and for His honor. God doesn't give us a dream that has to be compared to anyone else's. We are uniquely created and crafted, a one-of-a-kind masterpiece designed to complete the good works God lays in front of us—nothing less and nothing else.

By the grace of God, even our sins can be woven into God's dream for our lives. A teenage girl was in a relationship with an abusive boyfriend. She became pregnant and had to flee the state to get away from him. She felt shattered and alone, and she wondered if she had ruined her life. She had grown up in a home with parents who taught her about God's grace. Slowly, she remembered their messages, which gripped her heart.

> By the grace of God, even our sins can be woven into God's dream for our lives.

She had the child, got a job, and became a loving single mom. Her dream was to be the best mother her daughter could possibly have—and she has been exactly that. After several years, God brought a wonderful young man into her life, and today, they are happily married with three beautiful children. It's not hard to imagine how God is using this young mom. She's counseling unwed young mothers in her community, offering an arm of strength and a word of hope. The route to follow God's dream has been circuitous, but as she looks back, she can see His fingerprints all over her path.

What's Your Take?

1. How is *anointing* defined in this chapter? What does God's anointing look like in a person's life?

2. Would you say God has anointed you with a dream and His power to fulfill it? Why or why not?

3. What are some reasons humility is so rare? Who do you know who "thinks of himself less" instead of "thinks less of himself"? Is this attractive to you? Explain your answer.

4. What are some ways people are distracted by "continuous partial attention"? Is this a problem for you?

5. D. L. Moody often said, "It remains to be seen what God will do with a man who gives himself up wholly to him." Do you want to be that person? What are the risks and rewards?

6. How would you describe God's pruning? Is it really necessary? What are some reasons many of us resent it?

7. In what ways is Mary's story inspiring and challenging to you?

8. As you've read this chapter, what are some ways God might be gently correcting your perspectives about Him, your situation, and His dream for your life?

9. What is your next step in clarifying God's dream for you, trusting in His anointing, or cleaning out less-than-humble attitudes that block your progress?

Read together.

Prayer of Commitment

Lord God, You are the power of my dream. By Your Spirit, You anoint people to accomplish far more than they can do on their own. Lord, I'm Yours. Give me wisdom and direction. Prune me so I'll be more fruitful, and give me courage and tenacity to stay strong so I don't withdraw from the pruning process. Thank You for Your kindness, forgiveness, and strength. Amen.

3 The Doorway to Your Dream

I don't know what your destiny will be, but one thing I know: the only ones among you who will be really happy are those who will have sought and found how to serve.

—Albert Schweitzer, physician, winner of the Nobel Prize

In God's kingdom, there's no magic or pixie dust that makes dreams come true. Instead, the doorway to our dreams is selfless service.

Many years ago, late on a stormy night in Philadelphia, an elderly man escorted his wife into the lobby of a small hotel. They approached the clerk at the front desk and asked, "Could you possibly give us a room tonight?"

The clerk smiled at the couple but shook his head. He explained that three conventions were meeting in the city. He told them, "All of our rooms are taken." After a few seconds, he realized their plight and said, "But I can't send a nice couple like you out into the rain at one o'clock in the morning. Would you be willing to sleep in my room? It's not exactly a suite, but it will be good enough to make you folks comfortable for the night."

The couple politely declined his gracious offer, but he persisted, "Don't worry about me. I'll make out just fine."

The next morning the elderly man and his wife left the room and walked to the front desk. The man smiled and announced to the clerk, "You're the kind of manager who should be the boss of the best hotel in the country. Maybe one day I'll build one for you."

The clerk looked stunned, and then the three of them shared a good laugh. It was a grand and kind thought, but the clerk never expected to see them again.

Two years later, the clerk received a letter. When he opened it, he realized it was from the old traveler who had stayed in his room on that stormy night. The letter asked the young man to come to New York to see the couple. A round-trip train ticket was enclosed.

A few days later, the old man and his wife met the clerk and led him to Fifth Avenue and 34th Street. The man pointed to a magnificent new building of red stone with turrets and watchtowers. "That," the man intoned, "is the hotel I've built for you to manage."

The clerk was dumbfounded. He stammered, "You must be joking!"

With a wry smile, the old man replied, "I assure you I'm not. This is now your hotel."

The old gentleman's name was William Waldorf Astor, and the new hotel was named the Waldorf-Astoria Hotel. The kind young clerk whose service was noticed and valued was George C. Boldt, the first manager of the most magnificent hotel in the country.

A person with a servant's heart does whatever it takes to get the job done—without thought of convenience or applause. Servanthood opens the door to the fulfillment of a dream.

Living Inside Out

When we read the Gospels, one of the most striking observations is that Jesus consistently turned things upside-down and inside-out. He blew away people's expectations. In that culture (just like in ours), people valued beauty, wealth, and power. But who were the ones who responded to Jesus and experienced His love and acceptance? The outcasts, prostitutes, hated tax collectors, the blind, the lame, and the foreigners—not those on top of the cultural ladder: the religious leaders, the wealthy, and the powerful. Over and over again, we see this flip. Jesus welcomed a prostitute who experienced His forgiveness into the home of a smug, self-righteous Pharisee. A half-breed Samaritan was the hero of a story by helping a Jew who had been beaten and robbed, but two Jewish leaders refused to offer a hand. A tax collector, considered a traitor by the Jews, prayed at the temple next to a Pharisee. The Pharisee was confident that he was good enough to merit God's favor, but he was wrong. The contrite tax collector was the one who went away justified and forgiven by God.

To make sure He made His point crystal clear, Jesus explained this principle again on the night He was betrayed. After Jesus instituted the Lord's Supper and predicted His death yet again, His closest disciples began arguing about who would be the greatest. The scene would be comical if it weren't so poignant. The Son of God had stepped out of the majesty of heaven to suffer and die for us, but in His hour of need, His men jockeyed for position because they assumed the next day He was going to be made king and rule the world. They wanted to be sure to have the best positions in His cabinet. Luke paints the picture for us:

> *A dispute also arose among them as to which of them was considered to be greatest. Jesus said to them, "The kings of the Gentiles lord it over them; and those who exercise authority over them call themselves Benefactors. But you are not to be like that. Instead, the*

greatest among you should be like the youngest, and the one who rules like the one who serves. For who is greater, the one who is at the table or the one who serves? Is it not the one who is at the table? But I am among you as one who serves. You are those who have stood by me in my trials. And I confer on you a kingdom, just as my Father conferred one on me, so that you may eat and drink at my table in my kingdom and sit on thrones, judging the twelve tribes of Israel" (Luke 22:24–30).

We can draw a lot of truth out of that conversation, but one sentence stands out. Jesus told them, "But I am among you as one who serves." Did anyone ever deserve to be served more than God's Son, the Creator and Sustainer of the universe? But if He chose to humble himself to serve—to the point of death—what should our attitude and role be? Surely, if we intend to follow Jesus' example, we will become selfless servants, too. That night, Jesus demonstrated what it means to serve by picking up a towel and bowl of water to wash His disciples' feet (John 13:1–17). That was the role of the lowest servant in a home, and it showed the degree of selflessness Jesus wants for us. He told them to go and wash one another's feet.

Years ago, the church I pastored had endured tremendous conflict for many years before I arrived. Families were furious with other families, and there was conflict within many families. The church was a mess. I knew I couldn't talk our way out of this problem. Church members needed a tangible display of God's grace. The Lord led me to ask the leaders and staff to come for a meeting. This was a huge risk. I acknowledged the reality of the pain and anger in their lives, and I said, "I want to redefine leadership among us. We can't live with power struggles and resentment any longer." At that moment, Gail brought in some bowls of water and towels, and I went from person to person washing their feet. I looked up at each person and apologized for any hurt anyone in authority had caused them. The expression on each person's face changed from guarded anger to grateful love. No amount of teaching could have made the difference—only a tangible expression of loving, forgiving service. Serving each other opens the door to relationships. It breaks down barriers, melts hearts, and builds strong connections. Dreams are always about people, so a servant's heart is essential to fulfilling God's dream in our lives.

Being a servant turns our culture's values upside down, but it can only be achieved from the inside out. If we try to make it happen on our own, we'll be fakes, and we'll manipulate people instead of serving them. Make no mistake: the human heart is desperately wicked. We can do right things for very wrong reasons—to win approval, gain power, and snow those around us. The kind of serving Jesus calls us to practice finds its source in a full heart of love for God so that His kindness, compassion, and grace overflow from us into the lives of others. How can we tell if it's genuine? I think God gives us tests every day to see if we're truly servants. One of the most difficult is when people treat us like servants. When others don't appreciate our efforts, do we bristle with resentment? Do we gossip about them to get back at them? Do we sulk and withdraw? Or do we remind ourselves that we're really serving God, and He sees, He knows, and He values every act of service we perform—and that's enough praise for us.

> Being a servant turns our culture's values upside down, but it can only be achieved from the inside out.

Christ's love turns entitlement upside down. When we feel entitled, we demand honor, respect, praise, ease, resources, comfort, and anything else our hearts can desire. But no matter how much we get, it's never enough. Instead, in Christ we realize we not only have enough to fill our hearts, but far more. We actually deserved eternal condemnation, but we received eternal life; we deserved shame and blame, but we received forgiveness and acceptance; we deserved to be outcasts, but we were adopted into God's own family. A good grasp of the gospel fills our hearts, lowers our demands, and enables us to serve with no strings attached.

Who are the ones God calls to be servants? Every one of us—CEOs and janitors, doctors and gardeners, presidents and street sweepers. Even more, we find out if we're really servants within the walls of our homes. Whether we are fathers, mothers, grandparents, or kids, as we develop servant hearts, we look for ways to help one another instead of trying to get out of helping at all. Of course, some are more disposed to serve by temperament and personality than others, but all of us can learn to serve out of hearts full of gratitude.

Rebekah's Kindness

When Abraham was an old man, his son Isaac still wasn't married. He didn't want his son to marry any of the local women, so he sent his servant back to his homeland to find a wife for his son. The servant understood that his mission was vital to God's promise to bless the world though Abraham's son and his children. He left with ten camels full of valuables to give to the bride's family, a kind of reverse dowry. When he arrived in Nahor, he didn't know how to choose a wife for his master's son, so he prayed:

> LORD, *God of my master Abraham, make me successful today, and show kindness to my master Abraham. See, I am standing beside*

this spring, and the daughters of the townspeople are coming out to draw water. May it be that when I say to a young woman, "Please let down your jar that I may have a drink," and she says, "Drink, and I'll water your camels too"—let her be the one you have chosen for your servant Isaac. By this I will know that you have shown kindness to my master (Genesis 24:12–14).

Even before he finished his prayer, a beautiful young woman named Rebekah came to the well to draw water. The servant was so excited that he ran to her and said, "Please give me a little water from your jar."

After she gave him a drink, she told him, "'I'll draw water for your camels too, until they have had enough to drink.' So she quickly emptied her jar into the trough, ran back to the well to draw more water, and drew enough for all his camels" (Genesis 24:17, 19–20).

A camel can drink twenty-five gallons of water, so if the servant had brought ten camels, Rebekah cheerfully went back to the spring enough times to get 250 gallons of water for them! Without a doubt, the servant knew that such an act of kind service was exactly the sign he had been looking for. Rebekah was the one.

Abraham's servant introduced himself to Rebekah and asked to speak to her father. When they arrived at the father's tent and the servant told his story, Rebekah agreed to go with the servant to become Isaac's bride. Of course, when she offered to provide water for the camels that day, she had no idea she would receive such honor and blessing. She was simply doing what came from her heart—glad, kind, generous service for strangers, with no thought of reward.

Reboot

I love to be around people like Rebekah. They recharge my batteries, and they inspire me to serve gladly, too. But sadly, there are many people in our homes, businesses, and churches who serve, but with an edge of resentment. They may smile, but a closer look reveals a glint in their eyes and a tone of voice that says, "Yeah, I'm serving alright, and you'd better not forget it either!" For some reason, I think these people feel they are settling for second best. They see their role as second best, not God's divine placement. They feel that their work is worthless or unappreciated. Some feel like their role is their lot in life, a kind of prison sentence to be endured rather than an adventure to be explored. Sometimes, they've experienced significant disappointments, and they've given up. Maybe God took them through a time of pruning, but they didn't understand that He was going to resurrect their dream as more glorious and powerful than before—so they gave up on it. And maybe they were passive and let someone else define their dream for them many years ago. Resentment can come from many different sources.

Some of us were programmed with faulty data in our homes and, sadly, in our churches. We internalized information that only some roles are varsity level, and the rest of us are on the scrub team. To get rid of this mental virus, we need to download the truth from God's Word about His purposes, calling, will, and ways. We need to realize that every person in the Kingdom is essential. Paul taught the Corinthians that the members of the body that seem least important are crucial to God's design (1 Corinthians 12:22)

In several of Paul's letters, he talks about the importance of rebooting our minds to think rightly about God and our lives. In perhaps his most famous passage on this topic, he writes the Christians in Rome:

Therefore, I urge you, brothers and sisters, in view of God's mercy, to offer your bodies as a living sacrifice, holy and pleasing to God—this is your true and proper worship. Do not conform to the pattern of this world, but be transformed by the renewing of your mind. Then you will be able to test and approve what God's will is—his good, pleasing and perfect will (Romans 12:1–2).

Our minds aren't renewed by walking into the door of a church for an hour each week. It takes more than that. Think of what it takes to learn a new software program, a new golf swing, or how to play the guitar. Our minds are much more complicated machines than a computer, a golf club, or a musical instrument. Current research shows that brain function can be changed by creating new habits. Gradually, new neural pathways are formed, and new patterns of thinking and acting become second nature. Dive deep into God's word. Study, meditate, discuss, listen to messages, and memorize passages that mean a lot to you. Memorizing Scripture is like learning a song by your favorite singer. As you repeat it a few times, it becomes ingrained in your mind, and— *viola!*— you've memorized it.

Another way to bring joy into your service is to ask God for it. "The joy of the LORD is your strength" (Nehemiah 8:10), and God delights to give us joy. Trust Him to give you a new perspective on life, to change your heart so that you let go of the strings you've been trying to pull to control people and events. Take time to intentionally focus on the things God has done for you, in you, and through you. And sing your favorite song or hymn a couple of times each day. You'll be surprised how much these things can lift your spirit. Some people think that the Holy Spirit's work in the lives of believers is limited to tongues, signs,

> **I love to be around old people who are full of God's joy. They delight me, and even more, I'm sure they bring a smile to God's face.**

and wonders, but I disagree. One of the most significant manifestations of the presence and power of the Spirit is deep, lasting, profound joy—especially when times are tough. The more we're connected to the person of the Spirit, the more joy-filled we'll be. And some people think that old age is an excuse for becoming a curmudgeon. Oh no. The more we genuinely walk with God, the more we'll know the sweetness of God's kindness and compassion as the years wind down. I love to be around old people who are full of God's joy. They delight me, and even more, I'm sure they bring a smile to God's face.

Elaine Carlin was one of my favorites. As an elderly widow who never missed a church service, she had a contagious spirit. She was the kind of parishioner that I always made sure to greet. Elaine had an uncanny ability to make you feel good and smile. One Sunday morning, our student ministries worship team led the congregational worship. It was loud, and the songs weren't familiar to some of the people who preferred hymns. The worship service was quite a stretch for some of Elaine's peers, but immediately following the service, Elaine said to me, "Oh Pastor! Those kids were awesome! I couldn't quite understand all of their words, but I could tell they were passionate."

But infectious joy isn't the only factor that shapes our attitudes. To some degree, all of us are like sponges. We soak up the perspectives, attitudes, and behaviors of those around us. If we aren't careful, we can absorb the wrong things. Consider the people you hang out with and determine the impact they have on you. (Maybe they should do the same thing with you.) King Solomon wrote, "Walk with the wise and become wise, for a companion of fools suffers harm" (Proverbs 13:20).

Contentment and joy come from letting go of our demands and seeing ourselves as recipients of God's amazing grace. In Paul's letter to the Colossians, he addressed different people in the family: husbands, wives, parents, slaves, and masters. In his day, the slaves weren't chattel slaves, the kind we usually think of. Most of them were indentured servants who couldn't pay their bills so they sold their services for a few years. They weren't kidnapped, and they weren't beaten. They were sometimes leaders in churches where their masters attended. Still, being an indentured servant or slave was hard work. Paul reminded them,

> *Slaves, obey your earthly masters in everything; and do it, not only when their eye is on you and to curry their favor, but with sincerity of heart and reverence for the Lord. Whatever you do, work at it with all your heart, as working for the Lord, not for human masters, since you know that you will receive an inheritance from the Lord as a reward. It is the Lord Christ you are serving (Colossians 3:22–24).*

Notice that Paul said mere obedience isn't enough. It has to be fueled by a right heart and a clear head. All of us—employers and employees, parents and children, husbands and wives—need to remember that ultimately we serve God, and we live to please Him in everything we do.

Get Practical

Dreaming in 3D isn't just about grand and glorious challenges. God certainly may give us those, but He always wants us to serve those closest to us. Our true perceptions, desires, and commitments surface in the fabric of daily life, and we learn to become genuine servants in our relationships. I want to examine the essence of servanthood for fathers, mothers, managers, employees, and students.

A *father* and *husband* has inherent authority, so to be a servant, he refuses to exercise his power to get his own way. Some men throw down their power card and demand compliance—for everything from controlling the remote to choosing the restaurant to kids' grades to a wife's handling of money. But being a glorified dictator is a long way from glad and humble service. In four crucial relationships—with his wife, his children, his work, and his peers—men need to follow the example of Christ, who had all authority in heaven and on earth, but "emptied himself" to become a servant, even to ungrateful and unresponsive people (Philippians 2:6, NASB). Now, don't misunderstand. There are certainly times when a man has to stand up to speak truth into the lives of those he loves, and sometimes he has to hold them accountable. But these moments of correction go down a lot better if he's won their trust and affection by kindness, love, and affirmation. Paul told dads not to "exasperate" their kids—and spouses and neighbors and friends and everybody else (Ephesians 6:4). We exasperate people by being extreme: too demanding or too passive, too controlling or too distant. Many dads need to learn one simple but profound lesson, and it would change the atmosphere of their homes—to listen. Instead of being "the answer man" and dictating what each person thinks, says, and does, a man must learn to say, "Tell me more about what you're thinking." After people pick themselves off the floor, they just might tell him things about themselves he never knew before. Listening without correcting is a wonderful skill many dads and husbands need to learn.

Women who are *moms* and *wives* seem predisposed to display a servant's spirit in living color. They are often the ones who pitch in to help every member of the family, no matter what the need might be; and they offer to assist people in the neighborhood, at their kids' schools, and at church, too. The question for all these women is: Are there strings attached?

Luke's story of Mary and Martha depicts Martha as a tireless servant, but she cooked and cleaned with a chip on her shoulder (Luke 10:38–42). Her attitude is the polar opposite of Rebekah, who gladly did more than was expected of her as she got water for all the camels. Being a wife and mother is exhausting. Many women give gladly and selflessly for a long time, but they get worn down after a while. When "serving fatigue" sets in, little irritations grow into emotionally wrenching problems, and things that were no big deal now become cataclysmic. Jesus, the ultimate Servant, pulled away from the pressure and chaos of His life to regroup and recoup with His closest friends. Moms and wives—and all of us for that matter—need to follow His example by regularly carving out some time to refill our emotional, spiritual, and physical tanks. Sometimes, we are called on for extraordinary courage and service, but if we don't take time to recharge our batteries, we become tired and cynical. Contrary to the beliefs of some driven people, burnout is not a fruit of the Spirit! *Employers* and *managers* are in a position of authority. Like dads and husbands, they need to exercise their power with humility and grace. They are responsible for leading a company, a division, or a team, but job performance is only part of the equation. They need to remember that the men and women they lead are human beings, with real needs and desires, with dreams and dreads. In some cases, the company relationships are the most influential in an employee's life, so managers have the opportunity to make a profound impact for good. The news from the corporate world often tells horror stories of greed, abuse, and manipulation, but I believe that for every negative account there are a dozen unheralded examples of noble, compassionate, sharp business leaders who provide excellent leadership. These men and women value the people on their teams, and their team members know it. Mutual respect generates enthusiasm and creativity, and everyone thrives.

Some *employees* display a servant's spirit, gladly pitching in to accomplish the corporate goals, staying overtime to get the job done. But others are less than zealous for the cause. In Paul's second letter to the Christians in Thessalonica, he warned those who were bums. He wrote: "We hear that some among you are idle and disruptive. They are not busy; they are busybodies. Such people we command and urge in the Lord Jesus Christ to settle down and earn the food they eat. And as for you, brothers and sisters, never tire of doing what is good" (2 Thessalonians 3:11–13). Even then, Paul didn't give up on people. In the corporate world, we talk about instituting a standard of performance; in the spiritual world, we talk about giving people a second chance. Paul explained, "Take special note of anyone who does not obey our instruction in this letter. Do not associate with them, in order that they may feel ashamed. Yet do not regard them as an enemy, but warn them as you would a fellow believer" (verses 14,15).

Some people think that their job is beneath them, and others should respect them more. Martin Luther King Jr. knew something about respect. He led marches and movements to help raise the pay and working conditions for garbage workers, but he told them to do their work with dignity. He said:

> ...if it falls your lot to be a street sweeper in life, sweep streets like Raphael painted pictures. Sweep streets like Michelangelo carved marble. Sweep streets like Beethoven composed music. Sweep streets like Shakespeare wrote poetry. Sweep streets so well that all the hosts

of heaven and earth will have to pause and say, "Here lived a great street sweeper who swept his job well."[1]

Rebekah displayed this attitude. Twice in the Genesis account, it says that she "quickly" lowered the jar to get water for the servant's camels (24:18,20). She offered to do more than was expected, and she didn't complain that the work was too hard. She poured herself into her task and did it quickly and with a smile. Sometimes, of course, we need to sit back and do some analysis, but when it's time to act, we need to kick it in gear without delay. Rebekah made sure she accomplished the job even though the pay, conditions, and environment weren't pleasant. Camels are smelly animals. They snort and spit, and—to put it mildly—they aren't attractive. And they drink a lot of water. Rebekah could have found a dozen reasons why she didn't have to water them, but she valued selfless service more than personal convenience. That's the heart of a servant.

I'm not naïve. Some of us are in jobs that are very difficult. Sometimes working conditions are harsh. But more often and perhaps more challenging, some of us work under bosses who are inconsiderate, inconsistent, or incompetent. In these situations, we have to ask the Lord for wisdom. He may want us to stay, at least for a season, to learn important lessons or help others though the dark time. If we've gone to a supervisor with pure motives and the desire to try to resolve the problem, but keep hitting roadblocks, we may need to consider that the Lord might be leading us somewhere else. We need to be careful, though, to avoid expecting that the next job will be employment Nirvana. It won't be. Every job has difficulties. No matter what, we trust God to give us wisdom and grace so that we work hard—for Him if for no one else—and we see our difficult job situation as His classroom to teach us important lessons.

Like employees, *students* need to realize they are in a privileged position to soak up the blessings of their role. Yes, there are some teachers and professors who are very difficult, but the vast majority of them really care about their students and their field of study. They aren't the enemy. Most of the messages of pop culture say that teachers are stupid, oppressive oafs, and it's the goal of students to avoid learning at all costs. Some of these movies and television shows are very funny, but the not-so-subtle message is very destructive. Students need to see themselves as blessed people who are receiving the training and knowledge they'll need for a lifetime of effective living. As recipients of this blessing, they devote themselves to study and hard work with a grateful heart.

God Encounters

Everything in human nature and in our culture shouts a message quite different from servanthood. So how do we cultivate the attitude of one who serves? In Paul's letter to the Philippians, before he described Jesus as the ultimate example of a servant, he shined his light into the dark recesses of our hearts when he wrote, "Do nothing out of selfish ambition or vain conceit. Rather, in humility value others above yourselves, not looking to your own interests but each of you to the interests of the others" (Philippians 2:3,4). Why are we so ambitious? Because we long for glory and honor. Our hearts are empty, but we instinctively know we were created for a purpose. In our darkened minds, we look in the wrong places, pursuing fame, wealth, power, and pleasure. In the process, we become even more self-absorbed and use people to get what we want. The antidote is a powerful blend of insight and repentance. First, we need to see our selfishness for what it is—not just some random negative feelings, but a pervasive condition of our hearts that can only be changed by the grace and power of God. Until Christ fills our hearts with His love, we'll always do things for others with strings attached. We'll appear to be serving them, but in reality, it's all about us. For me, there have been many moments in my life when I encountered Christ in a fresh, life-changing way. Quite often, this encounter happens when the light of His Word shines on a dark place in my heart, and I turn to Him to be forgiven and changed. These encounters don't produce shame and guilt, but instead,

First, we need to see our selfishness for what it is—not just some random negative feelings, but a pervasive condition of our hearts that can only be changed by the grace and power of God. Until Christ fills our hearts with His love, we'll always do things for others with strings attached. We'll appear to be serving them, but in reality, it's all about us.

they remind me of Christ's overflowing, magnificent love, and they reinforce the dream more strongly than ever. The dream may have been high definition before, but now it's 3D.

Some of these God encounters have come in large, passionate worship services, but more often, they occur in private when the "still small voice" of God whispers to my heart (1 Kings 19:12). In these times, God recalibrates my spiritual GPS. I long for Him more deeply, I listen more intently, and I sense His strength more fully. I don't ever want to get to a place that I take God and His dream for granted. I expect Him to knock me down over and over again, to overwhelm me with His love, kindness, forgiveness, and direction time after time. I need those regular reminders of who God is and who I am as His dearly beloved child. Otherwise, I might take myself too seriously.

I really have a sense that time is short, and the Lord is coming back soon. Before He comes, I don't want to miss out on anything that He has for me. I don't want anything—even good things that aren't the best things—to distract me. I've seen some casualties of distractions. I've heard men and women smile wistfully and say, "I wish I could go back and capture God's dream for me again." Here's some great news: You can. It's never too late. We're only limited by our lack of imagination and lack of courage. There's still a dream out there to fulfill.

A servant's heart is the doorway to God's dream for our lives. The key to that door is a humble heart so filled with Christ that it crowds out doubt, passivity, and self-promotion. As God purifies our hearts, we are more attentive to His whisper, and the volume of our voice (and the voices of others) is turned down.

Do you sense the need to grow in humility? Join the club. Needing humility is part of the human condition. But you don't have to stay that way. Ask God for a close encounter with Him, and trust Him to turn your heart upside down and inside out by His great grace. He'll do it.

What's Your Take?

1. In what way is the gospel message "upside down" and "inside out"?

2. If you had been one of the disciples the night Jesus washed their feet, how would you have felt at the moment He washed yours? How would that moment have stuck with you for the rest of your life?

3. Think of the example of Rebekah at the well. What does it mean to serve others with no strings attached? What are some strings people use to get their way?

4. How can you tell if someone (maybe even you) is serving out of a full and overflowing heart, or if there's an edge of resentment?

5. What are some ways to bring joy into serving others?

6. In the section on practical applications, which points stood out to you? How will you make them real in your life?

7. Describe some God-encounters that have touched your heart. How are insight and repentance parts of these powerful moments?

8. What are some of the blessings and benefits of being a true servant, first of Christ and then of others around you? How does humility open the door to God's dream for your life?

Prayer of Commitment

Lord Jesus, You are the ultimate Servant. Help me, Jesus I want to follow You and be like You, but too often I engage in self-protection and self-promotion. Thank You for forgiving me. Make me more like Rebekah. Amen.

4 The Focus of a Dream

I learned this, at least, by my experiment: that if one

advances confidently in the direction of his dreams, and

endeavors to live the life which he has imagined, he will meet

with a success unexpected in common hours.

—Henry David Thoreau

People matter. Christ didn't die for a cause; He died for people. The focus of a God-given dream is never about the size of an organization, the wealth we earn, or the fame we gain from success. It's touching people's lives.

In an article in *The Wall Street Journal*, John A Murray shares a story that may surprise many of us. James Naismith wanted to be a preacher and tell people about Christ, but he realized that many people who needed the Lord never came to church. To connect with them, he took a job as a physical education instructor at the YMCA's International Training School for Christian Workers in Springfield, Massachusetts. His vision: "To win men for the Master through gym."

Naismith wanted to find or invent a game young men could play indoors during the harsh New England winters. He tested a number of outdoor sports and tried to tailor them to play indoors, but none of them worked. Murray wrote, "Finally, Naismith decided to draw from all of these sports: with a ball that could be easily handled, play that involved running and passing with no tackling, and a goal at each end of the floor." Naismith had invented basketball. He and YMCA director Luther Gulick insisted on good sportsmanship. Gulick wrote, "The game must be kept clean." He went on to say that Christian athletes should deplore "not merely ungentlemanly treatment of guests, but slugging and that which violates the elementary principles of morals."

For the next fifty years, basketball was one of the most effective evangelistic tools in America. In 1941, Naismith wrote, "Whenever I witness games in a church league, I feel that my vision, almost a half century ago, of the time when the Christian people would recognize the true value of athletics, has become a reality."[1]

Disordered Love

When the focus of our dream is on achievement and acclaim, we may climb high on the culture's ladder of success, but we will never be really satisfied. But when we long for God to use us to change a life, every step we help others take brings us great fulfillment. When Christ fills our hearts, He gives us a compassion transfusion, and we care about the things He cares about—people.

> So, the first step in getting our focus right is to rivet our hearts on Christ.

So, the first step in getting our focus right is to rivet our hearts on Christ. St. Augustine lived in the late fourth and early fifth centuries, but he had incredible insight into the human heart. He said our chief problem is disordered love. We love the wrong things too much. God has given us many things to enjoy, but they are secondary to knowing, loving, and serving Him. When we make secondary things into ultimate things, we short-circuit the Spirit's work in our hearts. Instead of following the *Shema* and loving God with all our hearts, we love beauty, money, food, sex, clothes, vacations, sports, or a hundred other things that are wonderful gifts, as long as we keep them in their right and secondary place.[2]

Paul told the Philippians, "For me, to live is Christ" (Philippians 1:21). Many people, including many Christians, put something else in Christ's place in that sentence. If we live for money, we become anxious when money runs out, and we drive ourselves to acquire more. If we live for people, what happens when they die or move away, or even when they frown at us? If we live for power, we feel threatened when others disagree with us. If we live for beauty, we worry when we see a wrinkle on our face or someone else with nicer clothes. We could fill in the blank with almost anything. Here's a problem: Disordered love isn't a minor inconvenience. We worship our ultimate value and use everything else to serve it. That's fine if our ultimate value is Christ, but if we make money, fame, power, sex, or anything else the ultimate value, we use God as a means to that end. We pray, not because we find God delightful, but because we want Him to give us what we want. We sing, give, and serve, not because we long to honor God, but because we want leverage so that He'll do what we want Him to. Disordered love is a big problem—the Bible calls idolatry. I'm not identifying this problem to condemn anyone, but only to show how easy it is to get off track. God has given us many wonderful gifts to enjoy, but let's be sure to keep those things in second place in our hearts. Only He deserves to sit on the throne there.

A conversation in the life of Jesus puts all this together.

A Lawyer's Questions

In the Gospel accounts, lawyers weren't the crafty characters of John Gresham's novels. They were religious leaders who were skilled in interpreting the Torah (God's Law) for the community. As Jesus traveled and taught, He stirred up tremendous controversy and confusion. He strongly upheld the Law, saying, "until heaven and earth disappear, not the smallest letter, not the least stroke of a pen, will by any means disappear from the Law" (Matthew 5:18). But in the same breath, He turned things upside down, saying, "You have heard that it was said to the people long ago… But I tell you…" (Matthew 5:21,22).

At one point, a lawyer asked Jesus the most fundamental question, "Teacher, what must I do to inherit eternal life?" (You can read the entire conversation in Luke 10:25–37.)Jesus answered with two parallel questions: "What is written in the Law? How do you read it?"

The lawyer knew the Law inside and out. He went back to God's command to Moses in Deuteronomy 6:5: "Love the Lord your God with all your heart and with all your soul and with all your strength and with all your mind." Then he added an ethical application from Leviticus 19:18: "Love your neighbor as yourself."

Jesus may have smiled, but He probably understood more about this man than the man wanted Him to know. Jesus answered, "You have answered correctly. Do this and you will live."

The lawyer wasn't finished, though. He asked, "And who is my neighbor?" Luke said he asked this question because "he wanted to justify himself." The Jewish leaders taught that to remain ceremonially clean observant Jews should not touch anything considered ceremonially unclean. The category of *unclean* included people the religious leaders considered "sinful," such as prostitutes and tax collectors;"defective," such as blind people or people with a disability; and "foreign," such as Samaritans and Gentiles. The lawyer's love was limited, and he wanted Jesus to confirm his limits.

Jesus used this moment to shatter the lawyer's conception of limits on compassion. He told them a story:

> A man was going down from Jerusalem to Jericho, when he was attacked by robbers. They stripped him of his clothes, beat him and went away, leaving him half dead. A priest happened to be going down the same road, and when he saw the man, he passed by on the other side. So too, a Levite, when he came to the place and saw him, passed by on the other side. But a Samaritan, as he traveled, came where the man was; and when he saw him, he took pity on him. He went to him and bandaged his wounds, pouring on oil and wine. Then he put the man on his own donkey, brought him to an inn and took care of him. The next day he took out two denarii and gave them to the innkeeper. "Look after him," he said, "and when I return, I will reimburse you for any extra expense you may have."

It's difficult for most of us to understand the shock this story caused when Jesus told it. The Jews of that time, especially their religious leaders, bitterly despised the Samaritans. The latter included the people who had come back from exile and intermarried with unbelievers (2 Kings 17:27–41). They were outcasts among outcasts. The racial discrimination our country experienced for many generations (and still exists in some hearts) is the closest approximation in our culture Jesus' cultural situation. The man who was beaten and robbed in Jesus' story was a Jew, but two Jewish leaders refused to lift a finger to help him. They were on their way to the temple, and to touch a dead person—he wasn't dead, but they assumed he was—would disqualify them from temple worship. The ceremonial law (to avoid touching the dead) and the moral law (to care for those in need) conflicted at this point. These two religious leaders valued the ceremonial law over the moral law. Why? I think it's because following the moral law requires more of our hearts, our time, and our resources. In other words, they valued convenience over compassion. To Jesus, though, God's dream is all about people—not rigid rules, not restrictions, and certainly not convenience. The Samaritan who stopped to help was a person the religious leaders hated, someone who commanded no respect from them. But he offered practical assistance in every way: he treated the victim's wounds, provided transportation, paid for shelter and food, gave him companionship during his time of need, and promised to pay even more if the expense of care increased.

Jesus' point was clear, challenging, and compelling: Too often, convenience severely limits our compassion. Jesus asked the probably stunned lawyer, "Which of these three do you think was a neighbor to the man who fell into the hands of the robbers?"

The lawyer replied accurately, "The one who had mercy on him."

Jesus probably nodded as He said, "Go and do likewise."

Compassion Is a Verb

For the Samaritan, compassion was a verb, not a noun. He took action. In contrast, the lawyer was one of those people who criticize men and women who are trying to help others, even as they themselves sit on the sidelines. But Christ refused to let this attorney narrow the identity of his neighbors. We have to watch out that we aren't like the lawyer. When God prompts a dream that takes us out of our comfort zone, we often rationalize the dream away. We shake our heads and mutter, "Well, that's not for me." If we follow Jesus, though, He'll push us, expand our hearts, and deepen our compassion for others.

Sympathy is feeling sorry for someone, but *empathy* is putting ourselves in their place, identifying with their pain and predicament. Empathy propels compassionate action. In his essay, "The Emotional Life of Our Lord," theologian B. B. Warfield identified the full range of emotions in Christ's life; but, he insisted, the Gospel writers described one emotion more than all the others combined—compassion.[3] Jesus' spirit moved, He was brokenhearted, and He wept over the pains and death people suffered. As we become more like Him, our hearts will break, too, and we'll take action to meet the needs of others.

A Broken Heart

Why aren't we more compassionate? I believe the sheer volume of information has overloaded us. We have become emotionally numb because we simply can't absorb it all. Jack Johnson's song, "The News," describes a mother's attempts to shield her child from the brutal and painful realities in the news. She tells her child that the death and destruction they see are just make-believe. Then she realizes something is missing in the telecast. She asks a piercing question:

Why don't the newscasters cry when they read about the people who die?
You'd think they could be decent enough to put just a tear in their eyes.[4]

I watch the news almost every night, but I'd crater if I let every image and every story get to my heart. As a defense mechanism, I've anesthetized myself somewhat to the pain and heartache I see. Why don't I have a tear in my eyes every time I watch the news on television, listen to it on the radio, or read it in the paper? If a friend told me about a loss like one of the tragedies in the media, or if I saw only one scene a week and let the horror sink in, I would cry for those who were hurting. For most of us, the overload of information from television news, radio, and newspapers is simply too much to absorb emotionally. We disconnect our souls from these painful images, and we are worse off for it.

If we let Him, God will break through our misconceptions and our insistence on convenience to melt our hearts. It happened to a man named Francis. He lived in a town in Umbria in northern Italy at the turn of the thirteenth century. His father was wealthy, and he spoiled his son. The boy wanted to be a knight. When his city went to war with a neighboring town, Francis joined the army, was captured, and spent a year in prison. As soon as he was released, he suffered a long illness, but his dream of becoming a knight was still strong.

He joined a troop of knights and bought fine clothes and armor. On the way to a fight, he met a shabbily dressed knight. Francis was touched by the appearance of the man who had fought in a noble cause, so he exchanged clothes with him. A short time later, God began working even more in the young man's heart. As Francis rode and prayed, he met a leper whose rancid sores horrified him. His compassion, though, overcame his revulsion. He jumped from his horse, gave the leper all his money, and then kissed his hand. That moment of spontaneous kindness transformed Francis's life. If God could help him love for this leper, he could love anyone. He visited the sick in hospitals and leper colonies, and he provided for beggars. Just as he had done with the shabby knight before, he exchanged his clothes with a beggar on the street. For the rest of his life, he gave the poor everything he could put his hands on. His life of faith, simplicity, and generosity was a beacon of light to people in a self-absorbed culture pursuing power, sex, and entertainment. His example of selfless love was so powerful that an entire movement began to emu-

When Christ lights a match in the heart of one person, the flame can grow into a wildfire of compassion.

late him. An order of new, compassionate leaders was established, and the Church (at least for a while) was revolutionized. We know him today as St. Francis of Assisi.

When Christ lights a match in the heart of one person, the flame can grow into a wildfire of compassion.

We can't care for *everyone*, but this solemn fact shouldn't prevent us from caring for *someone*. There are, of course, limits on our resources of time, money, and ability to help, but if our hearts aren't breaking on a consistent basis, we aren't following the model of Jesus. Caring for people, though, isn't all about suffering and death. Jesus was the most joyous person who ever lived. He delighted in the smallest expressions of faith, and He never felt guilty or acted compulsively to fix people's problems. He did the Father's will as He was filled with compassion, love, and joy.

In Jesus' story, the Samaritan was a neighbor to the man who had been beaten and left for death. Francis was a neighbor to the sick and poor. Luke's history of the early church tells us that some of our neighbors are right under our noses. In the first weeks after the Holy Spirit came at Pentecost, the new church was booming. The heartbreak of the weekend when Christ was crucified had been radically changed to amazement when He was raised from death. A few weeks later, the disciples were bringing people to personal faith in Christ as they told people in Jerusalem about Jesus.

Every day, Peter and John went to the temple to pray and preach, just as Jesus had done so many times before. One day, though, they noticed a crippled man near the gate. (You can read this story in Luke 3:1–10.) They followed the time-tested model of caring: to stop, look, listen, and touch. Peter looked at the man. He told him, "Look at us!" The man was a beggar, so he thought they were going to give him a coin or two. Instead, Peter said, "Silver or gold I do not have, but what I do have I give you. In the name of Jesus Christ of Nazareth, walk." Peter grabbed the man's hand, yanked him to his feet, and the man began jumping around to the delight of everyone who was watching! A moment of compassion changed a life, but it did more than that. Luke tells us, "When all the people saw him walking and praising God, they recognized him as the same man who used to sit begging at the temple gate called Beautiful, and they were filled with wonder and amazement at what had happened to him."

Here's a modern example of this kind of compassion: Mike Jenkins, the director of an inner-city youth program, boarded a flight to return home. In front of him, several men escorted a man in a wheelchair—he was paralyzed from his neck down. After shifting him to a seat and buckling him in, the men left the plane. Mike sat across the aisle from him. A little while later, the flight attendant served lunch. (This happened a few years before airlines instituted their austerity programs and stopped serving food.) She lowered the man's tray and put his plate in front of him. Mike noticed that the lady sitting next to the quadriplegic enjoyed her lunch, then folded her napkin and put her head back for a nap—while the crippled man looked longingly at his lunch.

Mike leaned over to the woman and asked if she was going to help him eat his lunch. To his surprise, she snarled, "He's not my responsibility. I don't even know him."

Mike was incensed. He rang the call button for the attendant. In a few seconds, she appeared. Mike pointed to the man and asked her, "Are you going to help this man eat his meal?"

She replied tartly, "Sir, it's not the policy of this airline to feed the passengers."

Mike was incredulous. He stood up and demanded that the woman sitting next to the man change places with him. She was shocked. "Why?" she asked.

"Lady," Mike was talking so loud that the whole plane heard him, "somebody has to *feed* him!"

She muttered some excuses and accusations as she picked up her purse and took her place in Mike's seat. Mike sat down next to the stunned man, smiled, and began tenderly feeding him his lunch. Tears rolled down the man's face as he ate. Mike's compassion for the man initially produced outrage at the fact that everyone near the man overlooked him. But it finally resulted in gentle, kind, loving action to help a man needed it.

We can be so preoccupied—with our self-absorbed disordered love or with a grandiose misunderstanding of God's dream for us—that we miss the people God puts in our path each day. If we open our eyes, we will see that the "obstacle" we've been stumbling over is God's dream for us to make a difference in people's lives. A little reflection goes a long way. Solomon noted, "A fool lets it all hang out; a sage quietly mulls it over" (Proverbs 29:11, *Message*).

Compassion Fatigue

The other side of caring deeply for people is a tendency to care too much for too long. Guilt may propel us to take action at the beginning, but it can't sustain us. We need to draw deeply and continuously on the love of Christ as our compelling motivation, and even then, we need to be careful that we don't become exhausted in helping others. Unless we take a break from time to time to regularly replenish our souls, we will experience burnout, sometimes called "compassion fatigue."

In his book, *Margin: Restoring Emotional, Physical, Financial and Time Reserves to Our Overloaded Lives,* Dr. Richard Swenson observes that stress at home and at work isn't our real problem. The real struggle comes from *too much* stress. Moderate levels of stress actually bring out the best in us because they stimulate our creativity and motivate us to accomplish bigger goals. But like the proverbial frog in the kettle, stress levels can rise gradually, and we don't even notice them. When high levels of stress become a normal condition for us, we become tense and irritable, we make dumb decisions, our sleep cycle is interrupted, and our relationships suffer. I know people who became self-righteous as they cared for others, looking down their noses at those who didn't care and serve as much as they did—which, in their view, was everybody. When we have this faulty perspective, anger and resentment slowly build up, and we experience physiological symptoms like headaches and stomach problems. At that point, we can experience the devastation of burnout.[5]

In caring for people with severe problems, we can experience a level of stress that can be compared to combat fatigue. In the Civil War, officers noticed that many soldiers became disoriented and ineffective under the prolonged strain of battle. The doctors of the day, however, didn't understand what was happening. A few decades later, during World War I, intense artillery bombardments caused thousands of soldiers to become emotionally and psychologically incapacitated, a condition called "shell shock." Finally, in World War II, high-ranking officers and doctors grasped the causes and impact of continuous combat. They noticed that the effectiveness of soldiers deteriorated when they were in combat more than ninety days during the entire course of the war. "Combat Exhaustion," a study by Army psychiatrists, showed that a soldier "became steadily less valuable [after ninety days in action] until he was completely useless."[6] The PBS documentary, *The Perilous Fight*, reported this about American soldiers in the Pacific theater: An astounding, "1,393,000 soldiers were treated for battle fatigue during World War II. Of all ground combat troops, 37% were discharged for psychiatric reasons."[7]

People who work in hospitals or other care facilities can suffer from "compassion fatigue," a mild form of post-traumatic stress disorder commonly associated with doctors, nurses, pastors, chaplains, and charity workers. Compassion fatigue can also affect non-professionals, such as family members, who provide care for their disabled children, chronically ill parents, depressed spouses, or mentally ill relatives. Those of us who provide such care, whether professionally or not, keep going day after day, pouring out our hearts, and working hard to meet needs because we're convinced that we're doing something valuable. But sometimes, we develop a "savior complex," thinking that we alone can shoulder the burden of a person's care. We need to be careful that we don't get out of balance in our care for others.

Keeping It Fresh

Caring for people can be draining. If we try to do it all on our own, we become exhausted, resentful, or both. But as Christians, we aren't left to our own devices. Before Jesus was

Caring for people can be draining. If we try to do it all on our own, we become exhausted, resentful, or both. But as Christians, we aren't left to our own devices.

crucified, He promised that God would send "another counselor" or "another advocate" in His place who would refresh us, empower us, lead us, and keep us connected to Him (John 14:16).[8] He was talking about the Holy Spirit. God's Spirit isn't an impersonal force, as Eastern mystics believe. He is the Third Person of the Trinity, co-equal with the Father and the Son, sent by the Father to dwell in our hearts, to remind us that we've been adopted by God, and to keep us on track with God's will. We simply can't fulfill God's dream without being filled by the overflow of the Holy Spirit's love and power.

I'm afraid the Church has experienced inappropriate teaching, unhealthy modeling, and confusing representations of the role of the Holy Spirit. These have caused many people to back away from the Spirit. The Holy Spirit's work in our life is far more than being the agent to produce certain speaking and sign gifts. Don't get me wrong, I believe in the Baptism of the Holy Spirit, and I also believe in the re-filling of the Holy Spirit. In his letter to the Ephesians, Paul tells them to "be filled with the Spirit" (Ephesians 5:18). The verb tense means "keep on being filled." The Baptism of the Holy Spirit was never intended to be a one-time, "I got it" experience. It's like a river flowing through us, or better yet, a strong, ongoing relationship with continuous conversation.

How does it work? When Jesus was in Jerusalem for a major feast, each day's ceremonial washings and sacrifices built to a crescendo on the final day. John explains:

On the last and greatest day of the festival, Jesus stood and said in a loud voice, "Let anyone who is thirsty come to me and drink. Whoever believes in me, as Scripture has said, rivers of living water will flow from within them." By this he meant the Spirit, whom those who believed in him were later to receive (John 7:37–39).

As we drink in and experience Christ's majesty, kindness, forgiveness, love, and wisdom, our hearts overflow with those traits so that we share them with others. That's one of the ways we can understand what it means to "be conformed to the image of [God's] Son" (Romans 8:29). Conformity is not a self-improvement plan based on rigid discipline; it's a vital, soul-satisfying, stimulating relationship with Jesus. That's what the Holy Spirit does in us and through us, and that's what it means to "keep on being filled with the Spirit."

As our Advocate representing us before the Father, the Holy Spirit assures us of God's love and reminds us that He rules over the affairs of men and nations. This assurance gives us real hope. As Paul concluded his magnificent letter to the Christians in Rome, he prayed, "May the God of hope fill you with all joy and peace as you trust in him, so that you may overflow with hope by the power of the Holy Spirit" (Romans 15:13). Earlier in the same letter, Paul reminded them they had a special relationship with God. He adopted us as His own, sending the Spirit into our hearts to continually remind us that we belong to Him. Then Paul explained the role of the Holy Spirit when we face difficulties and confusion:

In the same way, the Spirit helps us in our weakness. We do not know what we ought to pray for, but the Spirit himself intercedes for us through wordless groans. And he who searches our hearts knows the mind of the Spirit, because the Spirit intercedes for God's people in accordance with the will of God (Romans 8:26,27).

We may not know how to pray, but the Spirit does. We may not know God's will, but the Spirit knows. We can always have confidence that the Spirit of God knows, cares, and is praying to the Father for us.

God's dream for us is inaugurated by the Spirit of God, and it is confirmed by the Word of God and the people of God. The powerful interplay of these three give us hope, heart, and handles on the dream. They inspire us, correct us, and propel us to keep going when times are hard. At each step forward, we celebrate God's goodness and the incredible privilege of being His partner in the greatest enterprise the world has ever known—changing people's lives.

> **God's dream for us is inaugurated by the Spirit of God, and it is confirmed by the Word of God and the people of God.**

When I've faced times I didn't know how to respond—whether it was a career choice, a difficult conversation, a family issue, or anything else—these truths about the role of the Spirit have given me confidence in God. Being filled with the Spirit is not magic, and it's not weird; it's a vital relationship with Someone who loves me and stands outside of time, understanding the entire scope of God's will and ways. When I feel weak, I can trust Him and become strong. It's an amazing relationship. Quite often, the Spirit reminds me of a passage of Scripture that speaks powerfully to a current situation, and He illumines the text in ways I've never seen before so that His wisdom, love, and power become more real than ever. Through the loss of my dad, some difficulties in my career, and especially during a long time when Gail was sick, God's Spirit gave me "the peace of God, which transcends all understanding" (Philippians 4:7).

Our relationship with the Holy Spirit is a process, not an event. As we learn to listen to the Spirit's whisper, soak up the truth of His Word, and let the fruit of the Spirit become the scaffolding of our daily lives, we truly live the dream in 3D. This process, though, is a beautiful blend of the Spirit's activity and our obedience. In his book, *After You Believe*, N. T. Wright compares the process of spiritual growth with learning a new language.[9] We don't just jump on a plane, show up in New Delhi, and instantly know how to speak Hindi. We have to take the time to learn the vocabulary, sentence structure, and idioms of the language. After a while, we become conversant with people in India, and as we continue to master the language, we might even be mistaken for a native speaker. In our faith, learning the language of life requires discipline and determination, but we have the best Teacher the world has ever known, and the result of learning that language is that we find and fulfill the dream God uniquely created us to live. It's worth the effort.

Recipients of Compassion

Another layer of meaning in the story of the Good Samaritan is the symbolism of Christ as the Samaritan and we—you and I—as the man who was beaten and robbed. Before Christ came into our lives, we were helpless and hopeless. Others walked past us, but Jesus was moved by compassion to help us. He didn't just offer wine and oil for our wounds; He shed His own blood for us. He didn't just pay a few denarii to care for us; He paid with His life. He didn't just offer to pay for our food and board; He welcomes us into His eternal home in the new heaven and new earth. His compassion, kindness, and love know no bounds.

What does this mean? How does it affect the focus of people as central to our dream? The more our hearts are amazed with the grace of God, the more they will overflow with compassionate action for others. How much do we love others? John said that we love others to the extent that we have experienced Christ's love (1 John 4:11). Paul said that we forgive others only to the degree that we have experienced Christ's forgiveness for our sins (Ephesians 4:32), and we accept the unacceptable only if and when we realize Christ embraced us when we had nothing to offer Him (Romans 15:7). Genuine compassion can't be faked. It comes from a full heart, one touched by the Spirit and filled with the love, forgiveness, and acceptance of Christ. Then we will care for others with no strings attached. Then we'll be more like Jesus.

What's Your Take?

1. Why is it important that people (not success or fame or anything else) is the focus of our God-given dream?

2. How would you describe "disordered love"? How can your love become disordered? What are you doing about it?

3. In the story of the Good Samaritan, why did the lawyer want to justify himself? What are some ways we try to limit our involvement because it's inconvenient to care for people in need?

4. If you had been listening to Jesus story that day, how would you have felt and acted?

5. How would you describe "compassion fatigue"? Do you know anyone who has experienced it? What are some things we can do to prevent it (or recover from it)?

6. What are some reasonable limits to compassion? When is helping people actually hurting them (such as enabling an addict)?

7. How would you describe the Holy Spirit's role in the life of a believer? Was anything in this chapter about Him new or challenging to you?

8. On a scale of 0 (not at all) to 10 (completely), how much is the life of Christ overflowing from you by the power of the Spirit? Explain your answer. What are some ways you can "keep in step with the Spirit" even more (Galatians 5:25)?

Prayer of Commitment

Spirit of God, thank you for confirming my adoption into the family of God. I belong to you—it's amazing! I want to open my heart completely to You. Teach me, melt me, and mold me so that I take on more of the heart and life of Jesus. Break my heart with what breaks Yours. Fill me with compassion for hurting people, and give me courage to respond appropriately. Amen.

5 Dream Busters

What a man actually needs is not a tensionless state but rather the striving and struggling for some goal worthy of him. What he needs is not the discharge of tension at any cost, but the call of a potential meaning waiting to be fulfilled by him.

—Victor Frankl, psychiatrist and survivor of a Nazi concentration camp

Nobody likes suffering. In virtually all other eras of history, people expected to suffer as a normal part of life. But modern advances in medicine, technology, and communication have made life so easy for us that we expect to avoid difficulties and setbacks. If difficulties occur, we are shocked, and we think they should end immediately. But life doesn't work that way.

Dream Cycles

Many commentators have observed that a dream often goes through a predictable cycle of birth, death, and resurrection. The death of a dream, then, is a normal part of the progression. If we bail out of God's dream when we come to that point, we miss the glory of the resurrection. When dreams go backward, we need to have a long-term perspective. We need to understand that God is purifying our hearts, marshalling resources, or setting up His perfect timing to accomplish His good purposes. Difficulties don't mean that God has become our adversary. Just the opposite! He is our most gifted and diligent Teacher. He's committed to take us through the curriculum He has designed specifically for us so that we learn life's most important lessons. The things that appear to be dream busters are tests. Will we pass or will we fail?

Examples of the death of a dream are almost endless. My mother's world shattered when my father died. In a moment, her life changed from being the wife of a successful pastor to being a single mom. For a while, times were hard, but God gave her a dream of raising children to become competent adults. She could have wallowed in self-pity and tried to keep us kids under her thumb, but instead she gave us roots and wings. She launched us into the world with her blessing and encouragement to find and follow our own dreams.

A young couple, Richard and Suzanne, had a baby girl, Kimberly, but as soon as she was born, the doctor told her parents that something was wrong with her leg. An X-ray showed she was missing two bones in her left leg. For the next several years, the little girl endured a series of excruciating surgeries. Her parents cried as much as she did. Their initial hopes for their child crumbled to dust, but in the middle of prolonged procedures and much anguish, God gave them a different dream. Today, Kimberly is a mature, spunky, loving, popular student at a California university. She wears a lift shoe, but no one even notices. Richard said, "There were plenty of times Suzanne and I cried ourselves to sleep, but we kept going back to God—often to complain, always to pray. Early in Kimberly's life, we knew she wasn't going to be a regular, normal kid, so we asked the Lord to give us a special vision for her life. Today, her friends are amazed at her incredible self-concept. She loves God, loves people, and loves life. It wasn't what we wanted, but it's better than we could have ever dreamed."

Professor Ramesh Richard of Dallas Theological Seminary observed that a person's greatest heartache in his or her first forty years often becomes the foundation of ministry for the rest of life. I've seen that principle at work dozens of times. The woman who founded Mothers Against Drunk Driving (MADD) lost her child in an accident caused by a drunk driver. Many professional counselors went into the profession to help hurting people because they suffered abuse or abandonment in their own families. People who previously struggled through prolonged unemployment help others who are discouraged because they don't have jobs. A young woman diagnosed with multiple sclerosis has become a beacon of hope for others who suffer from physical illnesses and have lost hope in God and in their futures.

Paul explained this phenomenon in his second letter to the Corinthians:

Praise be to the God and Father of our Lord Jesus Christ, the Father of compassion and the God of all comfort, who comforts us in all our troubles, so that we can comfort those in any trouble with the comfort we ourselves receive from God. For just as we share abundantly in the sufferings of Christ, so also our comfort abounds through Christ. If we are distressed, it is for your comfort and salvation; if we are comforted, it is for your comfort, which produces in you patient endurance of the same sufferings we suffer (2 Corinthians 1:3–6).

Dream busters look like the end of the road, but if we trust God with them, we can experience a resurrected—purified, directed, and strengthened—dream. American revolutionary Thomas Paine wrote, "the harder the conflict, the more glorious the triumph. What we obtain too cheap, we esteem too lightly: it is dearness only that gives everything its value."[1]

The Big Three

At any point in the life cycle of a dream, but especially when it appears the dream is dead, we can be derailed by unresolved hurt, failure, or recurring sin. Let's take a look at these common dream busters:

Unresolved hurt

Everyone gets hurt from time to time. One of the most important skills we can learn, and sadly, one that too few have mastered, is the ability to resolve those wounds so we can move beyond them. I'm not minimizing the severity of those hurts. Some of us have experienced pains of enormous magnitude, including sexual and other types of abuse; violent crimes or natural disasters leading to post-traumatic stress disorder; and the emptiness, pain, and confusion of divorce. If we don't address these open wounds so they can heal, we take on the persona of a perpetual victim. The truth is that we've all been victims, but we don't have to remain victims. People who see themselves as victims become resentful and demanding. They live in a nightmare world of dark thoughts, longing for revenge and savoring every thought of hurting the one who hurt them. This deep resentment gives them two things

At any point in the life cycle of a dream, but especially when it appears the dream is dead, we can be derailed by unresolved hurt, failure, or recurring sin.

they value: identity and energy. They see themselves as the one who was wronged, so they feel completely justified in their self-pity and bitterness. And the longing for revenge fuels an adrenaline rush each day, which gives them enough energy to keep going.

This is no way to live. We need to learn to grieve and forgive. Grieving is the natural process of admitting the reality of the pain, facing it squarely, and resolving the hurt. Grief isn't just about death; it's about any kind of loss, including emotional and relational loss. When we refuse to face our pain, it remains in our hearts, festering and poisoning every thought and every relationship. The psalmist reminds us that God "heals the brokenhearted and binds up their wounds" (Psalm 147:3). The problem for many of us is that we never let our wounds heal. We pick our scabs, think about our hurts over and over again, and keeping them as open sores. This psalmist teaches us that God bandages our wounds so we can't keep picking at them.

Many (but not all) of our losses were caused by someone, and we need to forgive the perpetrator. Author Lewis Smedes had great insight about the importance of forgiveness. He wrote, "When we forgive evil we do not excuse it, we do not tolerate it, we do not smother it. We look the evil full in the face, call it what it is, let its horror shock and stun and enrage us, and only then do we forgive it."[2]

Forgiving those who hurt us is one of the hardest things we can ever do. Where does the courage to forgive come from? We have the power and motivation to forgive only because Christ has forgiven us. We draw deeply from the well of His forgiveness, and only then can we express His forgiveness to those who hurt us. Without this source, we only minimize the hurt ("It wasn't that bad"), excuse it ("He couldn't help it"), or deny it ("It didn't even happen"). Forgiveness sets us free from the prison of our bitterness. It doesn't necessarily mean, however, that we once again trust the one who hurt us. We forgive unilaterally—even if the person doesn't ask for it, even if he doesn't change, and even if he doesn't admit what he did. But reconciliation is a two-way street. We don't trust the person again until he has proven to be trustworthy.

Hurt is a very common experience, but it takes courage and insight to trust God, grieve, and forgive so those wounds don't ruin our lives. I'm convinced that some people experience chronic exhaustion because they use all their emotional energy on resentment and grudges created from past wounds. Quite often, the memories of those wounds continue to poison us for years, sometimes long after the offender has died. Smedes observed, "Forgiving does not erase the bitter past. A healed memory is not a deleted memory. Instead, forgiving what we cannot forget creates a new way to remember. We change the memory of our past into a hope for our future."[3] We simply can't remain stuck with a victim mentality and fulfill God's dream for us. The two are mutually exclusive.

Failure

Some of us are haunted by past failures. We may have failed sexually, morally, or ethically. We may have betrayed a close friend or our families. We may have done something terribly wrong only one time, but it was so demoralizing that it clouds our memories years later.

Some of us are perfectionists and believe that we should never ever experience failure. This unrealistic expectation sets us up to fail, and to be crushed by it. When we don't learn from failure and we let it color our lives too starkly, we become ashamed. There is a big difference between guilt and shame. We feel guilt because we've *done something bad*, but we feel ashamed because we've concluded *we are bad, unworthy people.* Guilt can be a very healthy response that leads us to repentance, but shame gnaws at us and leaves us feeling helpless, hopeless, and worthless. People may feel ashamed because they've failed so often, or they may acquire a pervasive negative self-evaluation because they failed miserably a single time. Either way, they feel their lives are effectively over, God has passed them by, and their dreams are dust.

When I enter any new role, I always tell people they can count on one thing: I'm going to fail, and they're going to fail, but I welcome the lessons we can all learn from our failures. Making a mistake isn't a cataclysmic blunder—unless we interpret it as the end of the world. I believe God sometimes allows failure to test us and give us a glimpse of what's in our hearts. Are we more concerned about our reputation or God's? Too often, we're far more interested in whether we look good in the eyes of others than whether God is honored or not.

One of the things I have to evaluate in times of failure is how much control I had in the situation. If the failure was out of my control, I don't worry much about it. But if I dropped the ball, I need to pay attention, listen well, and take corrective action. Sometimes, I made the best decision based on the information I had at the time. Again, I don't worry much if those choices don't work out well. But occasionally, I realize I pulled the trigger too quickly, and I should have asked a few more questions before I took a step. In any failure, I need to ask why it happened. The answer to that question determines my course of action.

I admire athletes who weave the lessons of failure into their careers. In sports, failure is very common. Baseball players who get a hit one-third of the time are destined for the Hall of Fame. Quarterbacks who complete half their passes are proven winners. In almost every sport, people who are perfectionists don't last long. Michael Jordan, arguably the greatest basketball player who ever lived, commented, "I've missed more than nine thousand shots in my career. I've lost almost three hundred games. Twenty-six times I've been trusted to take the game winning shot…and missed. I've failed over and over and over again in my life. And that is why I succeed."[4]

The way parents respond to failure—their own and their kids'— shapes a child's life in powerful ways. I've seen adults who still suffer from the abuse they endured growing up. Their harsh, critical, condemning parents blew up when they didn't meet their parents' impossibly high standards at school, around the house, or in any other way. But I've also seen plenty of strong, mature, wise people who point back to the way their parents helped them process the inevitable failures of childhood— especially adolescence. Their parents had standards, too, but they had a very different way of responding to failure. They calmly and lovingly pointed out the flaw and asked, "Now, what can you do next time?" How parents respond to their children's failures makes all the difference in the world to those kids.

One of the best things a parent can do is model confession and repentance when they fail. A few years ago, when our girls were younger and I was a pastor, our family drove to a gym to work out. In the parking lot, I waited for a car to back out of a space. I had my turn signal on to let everyone know I was going to park in that space. As the lady pulled out, a guy in another car quickly pulled in before I could get there. I was furious. I pulled behind him and stopped. He got out and stormed toward me. I got out, and we began jawing at each other as Gail and the girls watched. Finally, I got back in and parked somewhere else. As I worked out that day, I felt terrible about the example I had set for my family.

When we left, I said, "Let's go get a smoothie. I want to talk to you." We sat down in a little restaurant, and I told them, "I'm so sorry for the way I acted when that car pulled into the space in front of us. It was dumb and immature. Will you forgive me?"

They nodded, but Kaylee said, "Dad, I forgive you, but I really think you should have punched him in the nose." (She's her mom's girl.)

Even today, many years later, the girls sometimes refer back to the events of that day. The fact that I made such a mistake isn't a big deal to them anymore, but it's a very big deal that I admitted what I did and apologized. They remember my apology like it happened yesterday.

Recurring sin

While we're on this side of the dirt, we're not going to live a sinless life. Our response to our sins, though, determines whether our dream remains 3D and in vivid color or fades to black and white. The Scriptures contain many different vice lists. These include overt, destructive behaviors as well as hidden matters of the heart. Either way, "the wages of sin is death," creating a barrier between God and us (Romans 6:23). Even for those who have been born again, sin hardens our hearts and causes problems in all of our relationships—unless we practice confession and repentance. Most of us do a pretty good job of hiding our sins. We may have done unspeakable things to each other as we got ready for church, but the moment we get out of our cars in the parking lot on Sunday morning, we look like we've stepped out of a Norman Rockwell painting—all sweetness and light. No one knows about our lies, gossip, or porn addiction. But if they look closely, they might see lines in our faces that give away the reality of our hurt, bitterness, and self-righteousness. And if they take a glance at our families, they might see traces of frowns or tears of unhappiness. And of course, we do a great job hiding sins of cowardice, self-pity, greed, self-sufficiency, and jealousy. For all of these, we easily explain them away and insist, "They're no big deal." In many cases, we actually feel that we can justify our sinful attitudes and actions.

The presence of sin doesn't disqualify us from achieving our dreams, but letting our sins fester certainly can.

The presence of sin doesn't disqualify us from achieving our dreams, but letting our sins fester certainly can. Paul was under no illusions about the reality of sin in our lives. In his letter to the Galatians, he said we're in a fight:

> So I say, walk by the Spirit, and you will not gratify the desires of the flesh. For the flesh desires what is contrary to the Spirit, and the Spirit what is contrary to the flesh. They are in conflict with each other, so that you are not to do whatever you want. But if you are led by the Spirit, you are not under the law (Galatians 5:16–18).

Temptation isn't sin, but giving in to it is. Every temptation is a test to check our hearts to see what we value most. In each test, we can see where our love and loyalty lie. Do we want to please God, or do we care only about pleasing ourselves? Each temptation, then, is an opportunity to remember the wondrous grace of God, to rekindle the passion of our heart, and to love God with all our heart, soul, mind, and strength.

When we sin, we face a choice. God has provided the ultimate solution for sin. Christ died for all our sins—past, present, and future. We can wallow in shame, or we can gladly embrace His forgiveness. Paul explains two kinds of repentance to the Corinthians. One kind focuses on our ability to make things right on our own by feeling bad enough, long enough—a form of penance. I've known many people who thought God wanted them to grovel in shame for a period of time before they could know they were forgiven. The problem was that they did something else sinful while they were groveling, so they had two things to resolve, and then three or four or five. But Christ has already paid for our sins. He opened the door to the prison and set us free. In his first letter to the Christians in Corinth, Paul confronted them for several sins. Before he wrote his second letter, he got good news about their response:

Even if I caused you sorrow by my letter, I do not regret it. Though I did regret it—I see that my letter hurt you, but only for a little while—yet now I am happy, not because you were made sorry, but because your sorrow led you to repentance. For you became sorrowful as God intended and so were not harmed in any way by us. Godly sorrow brings repentance that leads to salvation and leaves no regret, but worldly sorrow brings death (2 Corinthians 7:8–10).

Do you see the difference? Godly sorrow points us to Christ, refreshes our spirits, and reminds us of His grace. But worldly sorrow (what we call shame) crushes our spirits and leaves us feeling helpless and hopeless.

Confession is agreeing with God about our sin, about His forgiveness, and about our new direction to honor Him. John gave us this wonderful assurance, "If we confess our sins, he is faithful and just and will forgive us our sins and purify us from all unrighteousness" (1 John 1:9). Recurring sin is slavery. It oppresses us and kills our dreams, but God's gracious forgiveness restores us and renews the dream—even better than it was before.

Why, we might ask, do people remain stuck in hurt, failure, and recurring sins when Christ has a remedy for them? I believe there are several possible reasons. Staying stuck enables people to avoid painful facts and hard choices. Remaining mired in a victim mentality gives them attention as "the poor, pitiful person who was wronged." Thoughts of revenge give them a surge of energy, and feelings of hopelessness prevent them from moving ahead with courage and tenacity. And besides, it's a lot easier to blame others for our past than to take responsibility for our future.

> **It's a lot easier to blame others for our past than to take responsibility for our future.**

Seizing the Moment

If anyone had an excuse to stay stuck in a dreamless life, the blind man Bartimaeus certainly did. But past and current difficulties couldn't prevent him from dreaming in 3D. Mark 10:36–42 tells us the story: "Then they came to Jericho. As Jesus and his disciples, together with a large crowd, were leaving the city, a blind man, Bartimaeus (which means 'son of Timaeus'), was sitting by the roadside begging. When he heard that it was Jesus of Nazareth, he began to shout, 'Jesus, Son of David, have mercy on me!'"

People around him were annoyed and told him to be quiet, but he refused to shut up. He raised the decibel level of his cry: "Son of David, have mercy on me!"

One person, though, wasn't annoyed at all. Jesus stopped and called for the blind man to come over. The people who had been telling Bartimaeus to be quiet probably shook their heads in disbelief as they told him, "Cheer up! On your feet! He's calling you." He jumped up, threw away his cloak, and stumbled over to Jesus.

I love the fact that Jesus wasn't codependent. He could see that Bartimaeus was blind, but He didn't jump in to fix his problem without being invited. He asked the man, "What do you want me to do for you?"

Bartimaeus answered, "Rabbi, I want to see."

"Go," said Jesus, "your faith has healed you." At that moment, he could see. He began following Jesus on the road.

Bartimaeus is a terrific example of someone who refused to lose. He didn't let a debilitating condition rob him of his dream, and he didn't listen to those around him who said his situation was hopeless. We don't know how long he had been begging, but certainly for many years. Now, when the opportunity appeared, Bartimaeus seized the moment. Some of us see an opportunity, but we say, "Well, I'll catch it next time." But Jesus never came back on that road to Jericho. There would never be another opportunity for Bartimaeus. The opportunity is now or never, and for Bartimaeus, it was now. If we wait for the ideal time to deal with dream busters of hurts, failures, or recurring sins, we might miss the best opportunity of our lives.

Never Give Up

In 1924, British climber George Mallory was asked why he wanted to climb Mt. Everest, the tallest and most daunting mountain in the world. At the time, no one had ever climbed Everest. Mallory replied with eloquent simplicity, "Because it's there."[5] In the past century, climbing the world's highest mountains has become an obsession for a few brave men and women. They don't climb for fame or fortune. They challenge themselves to push past the limits of physical and psychological endurance, to stare death in the face and take another step.

When she was twenty-one years old, Stacy Allison caught the bug. On her first significant climb on Mt. Huntington in Alaska, she was only two hundred feet from the top when her partner's ice ax broke. They were forced to turn around, brokenhearted but even more determined to reach the top of as many peaks as possible. She reflected, "Our ability to respond positively to setbacks fuels our creativity and lays the foundation for future successes."[6]

The next year, Stacy reached the top of Mt. McKinley, the tallest mountain in North America, and she joined a team of women to climb Ama Dablam, Nepal's 22,495-foot peak. But these exploits were only preparation for the ultimate challenge—Mt. Everest. She joined the North Face Expedition, but she failed to reach the top. She and her fellow climbers were caught in the worst storm on the mountain in forty years, and they were trapped in a snow cave at 23,500 feet for five days. Stacy again faced the reality of failure, and she paid a steep price in time, effort, and resources. But she learned a valuable lesson about persistence and tenacity.

Stacy simply wouldn't quit. She returned to Mt. Everest with a different team, the Northwest American Everest Expedition. After climbing from base camp to base camp for twenty-nine days and a final push to the top, Stacy became the first American woman to reach the top of the world at 29,028 feet.

Later, she led teams up the slopes of K2, thought by many to be the most difficult mountain in the world to climb. As a leader, she valued each person as much or more than the goal of getting to the top. On one of these expeditions, three of the seven members of the team reached the top, but injury to one caused the entire team to stop and head back down the mountain.

Thousands of people hike the Appalachian Trail every year, and thousands more hike in the Rockies, the Cascades, and other ranges. Mountain climbing, however, is significantly different. Mistakes on hiking trails lead to blisters; mistakes on Everest can end in death. The few dedicated climbers who try to climb the world's highest mountains endure excruciating training and invest time and money to participate in an expedition. When they finally arrive in Nepal or Tibet, they're just beginning. They face weeks—if not months—of additional preparations to gather resources and set up one base camp after another. The elevations are so difficult on the human body that climbers have to become acclimated to each camp for several days before they can make the next climb. All the work produces stories of triumph and tragedy. Those who climb to the top of the world experience painful moments of self-doubt and conflict with team members because oxygen-starved brains muddy their minds and choices. Still, these people are driven to accomplish the seemingly impossible. They face the probability of failure, but nothing can stop them. They have that rare commodity—courage.

The lessons Stacy Allison learned in climbing translate to every arena in life. She refused to let potential dream busters deter her from her goals. She has written two books, *Beyond The Limits: A Woman's Triumph on Everest* and *Many Mountains to Climb: Reflections on Competence, Courage and Commitment.*[7] She explains the principles she applies to overcoming every struggle. The difficulties we all face, she is certain, will make or break us. As the philosopher said, "What doesn't kill us makes us stronger." Stacy reflected on her role as a team builder, "In any endeavor, leaders should inspire members of the team with a passion for success, but within the framework of team effort. One of the most crucial things to realize, feel and remember is that when one team member succeeds, the entire team succeeds."[8]

We can always find excuses to let our dreams wither and vanish. We can look at past failures or current setbacks and assume that it's hopeless.

Bartimaeus and Stacy Allison refused to let anything stand in their way. What's your excuse?

What's Your Take?

1. Have you seen anyone (maybe yourself) experience the natural cycle of a dream—birth, death, and resurrection? Describe what happened?

2. What are some reasons people give up when they experience the death of a dream instead of hanging on for the glorious resurrection?

3. How would you define and describe a victim mentality? How does it poison our thoughts, our outlook, and our relationships?

4. What's the difference between guilt and shame? How can we effectively handle failure so that it doesn't crush us?

5. Why do many people live with recurring sins instead of repenting and experiencing Christ's forgiveness, cleansing, and freedom? What are they missing by refusing to confess and repent? What advice would you give them? Do you need to take your own advice? Explain your answer.

6. What are some ways Bartimaeus is a terrific example of someone who had the courage to face his dream busters? How can you emulate him?

7. As you've read this chapter, has the Holy Spirit pointed out any excuses you've used to let dream busters prevent you from finding and fulfilling God's dream for your life? If so, what are they? What are you going to do about them?

Prayer of Commitment

Lord Jesus, You suffered the ultimate death of a dream, but You were raised from death to life! You faced the death part of this cycle with incredible grace and courage. Give me courage to face my fears, overcome my excuses, and press on to be the person You want me to be. Thank You for being my strength in moments of weakness. Amen.

Dream Releasers

Keep away from people who try to belittle your ambitions. Small people always do that, but the really great make you feel that you, too, can become great.

—Mark Twain

Dreamers attract dreamers, and complainers attract complainers—it's a law of human nature. Through the years, I've watched men and women who reached for the stars. Others who were hungry for their lives to count wanted to hang out with them, ask them questions, watch them work, and pattern their lives after them. But I've also seen groups of gripers, clusters of people whose common goal was to outdo each other in finding fault with anyone and everyone. I try to avoid these people like the plague.

Very few people fulfill their dreams solo. Even in individual sports like golf, successful people have a team behind them: coaches, advisors, cheerleaders, supporters, and helpers of all stripes. A few Lone Rangers become quite successful, but it's not part of God's plan. He created us in His image as relational creatures. In the Trinity, the Father, Son and Holy Spirit love each other and work to accomplish Their unified purposes. God wants us, His Body, to work together to fulfill the dreams He puts on our hearts. We are far more effective when we work together…and it's a lot more fun, too.

My Team

After my father died, God brought some people into my life who saw me for who I could be, not just who I was. As God's dream for me unfolded, these people played important roles in shaping it and providing resources for it to become a reality. Most of these people aren't superstars. They're just ordinary men and women God used in an extraordinary way—men like Mike Tidswell, my Sunday School teacher, Dave McKelvey, my Royal Ranger commander, and Gary McMunn, a farmer who was my first employee. They were surrogate fathers who took time for me, looked into my eyes to speak messages of affirmation and love, and patiently pointed me toward God's dream. When they taught the Scriptures, especially the Gospels, they captivated my mind and my heart. Don't misunderstand. I wasn't a young Bible scholar by any means. I was a typical, squirrelly, note-passing, gum-chewing, rambunctious preacher's kid. They could have looked past me very easily, but they didn't. God gave them eyes to see potential when most people would have required a microscope to see any in me.

During those years, a recurring message I heard from many different sources was: "Doug, God has a plan for your life." Gradually, I began to believe it.

When I was a sophomore in high school, I was particularly moved during a missions service. A dear couple, Allen and Verna Bailey, noticed that God had touched my heart. They came over to talk with me, and I told them that I felt God's continued affirmation to pursue full-time

Christian vocational ministry. A week later, the Baileys found me at church and told me God had put it on their hearts to help pay for my college education. My mother certainly didn't have a wad of money to send me to school, but the Baileys became "dream releasers" who noticed God at work in me and dove in headfirst to provide resources for me. Talk about strategically investing in the next generation!

When I was in college, I was asked to speak at our school's senior class chapel. I hadn't done much formal speaking, so I wanted to be well prepared. I spent countless hours on my message, looking up points, finding great quotes, memorizing stories and transitions. I was ready. But when I walked up to the pulpit, I became a quivering mass of jelly— mentally and physically. I had a hard time remembering *what* I wanted to say, and I completely forgot *how* I wanted to say it. All those hours of preparation just evaporated. My twenty-minute talk was over in nine minutes. At the end, I gave an invitation, but no one came forward. When the service was over and people began leaving, I was devastated. If this was any indication of my speaking ability, I needed to find a job as a plumber, farmer, or electrician! As people walked out and I sat in my dejection, Dr. Gary McGee put his arm around me and said, "Doug, thank you so much for your message. It's so refreshing not to have to listen to a marathon sermon in our chapel!" His kindness meant the world to me at that moment.

When I began my pastoral career, I knew that I didn't want to try to build a personality-driven ministry. Some people might be tempted to do that, but I knew better. One of God's greatest gifts to me during those early years was a team of deacons at our church who were sharper than me, were infinitely patient with me, and refused to participate in power struggles that often tear churches apart. The faces of Greg Shapiro, Dan

Vandervlucht, Jim Keller, and Don Svenby are permanent fixtures in my mind.. Their attitudes about life and their perspectives about leading as a team gave me a huge head start in shaping my leadership philosophy. They delighted in seeing God work, and they didn't care one whit who got credit for it—as long as God got most of the applause.

As I look back on my life, finding and fulfilling God's dream hasn't been an accident. At every crucial point, God has brought people into my life to affirm His calling, clarify my direction, correct me when I was drifting, and challenge me to always go higher and farther than I ever dreamed possible. Sometimes, they've been God's pruning shears to say hard things to me, and sometimes, they've kept me out of big trouble. The church where I pastored was in a world of financial hurt when I arrived. After spending some time to assess the situation and work on a plan, I told our deacon board that I wanted to assemble a financial management team. They thought this was a good idea, but when I listed the names of the people I was recommending, they had problems with one of the men I suggested. One of the deacons said, "Pastor Doug, he isn't a member of the church."

I retorted, "Yes, but he's a very sharp financial manager, and I think we need him."

I hoped that would be enough to win the debate, but it wasn't. The deacons were firm in their requirement that the people on this new team be church members. I had made a commitment not to pick dumb fights with the deacons, so I agreed to their requirement. I agreed on the outside, but inside I was fuming. I thought it was unfair, narrow, and unwise not to use the talents of people God had put in our church's orbit. Then, three weeks later, I opened the newspaper and read that the man I had wanted on our financial management team had been a part of a high profile lawsuit, and it was potentially one of the biggest real estate scandals in the city's history. He was at the center of all this controversy.

At our next deacons' meeting, the others didn't say a word—they didn't have to. I thanked them for their wisdom and tenacity to stand up for what they saw was right. I learned a big lesson that day: to be a better listener, especially when people disagree with me. Eventually, the man I had recommended suffered a traumatic divorce, had a very tainted reputation in the community, and left the church.

The person I've learned to listen to most intently is my wife. Gail has wonderful insights, and if I'm smart, I listen carefully to her perspective. Not long ago after a dinner conversation with a colleague, she stopped me, "You may not be aware of it, but you controlled the conversation tonight far too much."

As usual, I looked perplexed, so she explained, "You're very good at asking questions and drawing people out, but sometimes, people want to ask you questions. Tonight, you kept asking questions and dominating the direction of our time together. If you'd been quiet for a minute, you'd realize he had some needs he wanted you to meet. Too bad you missed it." Ouch! Gail's words hurt, but as I thought back about the dinner, I knew she was right.

Consider the Content

There have been times in the past when I was defensive when people said hard things to me, but over they years, I've learned that God often uses correction in powerful and productive ways to keep me on track with His dream. Some people say, "Yeah, but consider the source!" I disagree. I want to first consider the content of the message. Quite often, there's truth in the message even when the messenger is less than loving in the delivery. God can use anyone at anytime to give us an important directive. After all, He used Balaam's donkey to speak truth to the prophet (Numbers 22:21–41). If He can use a donkey, He can use the people in our lives (even if they sometimes act like donkeys) to give us insight and guidance.

In the areas of my life where I want to grow, I've come to expect God to use people to give me words of correction as well as affirmation. Maybe I used to be surprised and defensive when someone told me something I didn't want to hear, but today I welcome such input. Many people are fragile and defensive. They spend a lot of their emotional energy protecting themselves from any correction because they take it so hard. As we become more secure in God's love, we'll be able to relax, not take ourselves so seriously, and welcome correction that can make us better people—no matter the source. In fact, I've become suspicious of "happy talk," the always-pleasant banter that only skims the surface of human connections. Certainly, we can encourage one another deeply, for genuine affirmation isn't superficial. It notices character, not just behavior; it focuses on a person's deepest desires, not just the visible results of his or her actions. That's the kind of impact Dr. McGee had on me that day when I spoke in chapel. He looked far beneath the surface. He saw into my heart, and he affirmed me deeply and specifically. Solomon wrote about the importance of being genuine: "Wounds from a friend can be trusted, but an enemy multiplies kisses" (Proverbs 27:6).

Guys and Dolls

In marriages, in businesses, and on teams in every organization, men and women often approach life quite differently. We can't make categorical distinctions, but we can certainly point out patterns that affect how each gender typically relates to others. It can be helpful to identify these. A little understanding goes a long way to facilitate better communication.

A very loving mom raised me, so I have great appreciation for the unique qualities of female communication. Women tend to be compassionate, caring, tender, and warm. In marriages and on teams, most women are more intentional about establishing and protecting relationships than are men. Men, on the other hand, often feel driven to get the job done, even at the expense of the people around them.

Studies of the brains of men and women have found that the actual brain function of the genders is significantly different. Women have a larger limbic system in their brains than men. This part of the brain enables them to be more in touch with the full range of their emotions and promotes bonding with others, including their spouse, children, friends, and peers at work. Unfortunately, this feature also makes them more susceptible to an overload of emotions, which can lead to depression, especially during particularly stressful times in their lives. The amygdala is another important feature of the brain for men and women. In men, the right amygdala is activated in response to pain, the side that controls external functioning and behavior. In women, the left side, which controls internal functions, is activated, which explains why women perceive pain more intensely than men. When a man shakes his head and says, "Just get over it," his wife can say, "My brain is telling me this is serious!"[1]

Women are more gifted in communication skills, and they generally look for solutions that work for the whole group, not just for themselves. Women can pick up on non-verbal cues and discern how people are doing without them saying a word, but men typically don't perceive another person's emotions unless and until they are stated explicitly. Men tend to think with the left side of their brains, so their approach to situations is to compartmentalize and solve isolated problems. In contrast, women use both sides of their brains. They are as creative as they are disciplined in finding solutions.

In response to conflict, men have a "fight or flight" reaction. Women often approach tense situations in a very different way. Psychologist Shelley E. Taylor observed that women use a "tend and befriend" strategy.[2] For example, a mom under stress fiercely protects her children and herself (tending), and she utilizes strong friendships for support and resources (befriending). Though women are often more caring, they can also be quite critical. They have high expectations for those they love, and those expectations can be seen as demands by others. Men are less comfortable with talking about feelings and meaning in relationships. They can talk all day about sports, tools, fishing, or spreadsheets, but when asked about their feelings, many of them don't have a clue what to say.

How Do I Look?

In most relationships, men are all about image management. They don't want anyone to see any flaws at all, so they're careful to project stability and proficiency in all things. Their motto is, "Never let 'em see you sweat." This may work well in a boardroom, but it creates distance in the bedroom and at the dinner table. Men need to find their security in Christ so they can let their guard down, be real human beings, and experience the joy of genuine connections. If they can find some people—maybe only one—who will accept them for who they are, they can find more peace, stability, creativity, and love than they ever imagined.

Big differences are seen in the generations, not only in the genders. Men from the Builder or Boomer Generations focus on accomplishments, and they often aren't willing to be vulnerable with others. Today's young people, though, value authenticity. If those around them are too self-protective, these young people don't trust them very much. Older people are impressed with the size of a person's dream, but the younger generation is looking for the authenticity of a dreamer's heart.

Can You Hear Me Now?

What difference does it make to understand gender and generational differences? It can make a world of difference in how well we listen to others and how much we trust others. When we feel understood, the world opens up to us, but when we feel isolated and alone, we become timid or angry—or both. There are, then, two points I want to make. First, understand yourself. Realize your strengths and shortcomings in communication, as a man or woman and as a younger or older person. Realize that you see life through a particular lens, and your brain structure and chemistry is quite different from your spouse and others around you. When your husband or wife doesn't "get" you, don't take it personally. Try to connect on his or her wavelength, and be thrilled when you see progress, or even some desire to understand. Second, understand those around you. Realize they may not be wired the same way you are. Don't try to force them into your mold. God created us with different physiques, different perceptions, and different reactions. "Different" isn't a value statement, so avoid being judgmental. Above all, learn the art of listening without condemning. I can always tell I'm really listening if I ask a second or third question instead of thinking about the next thing I want to say.

> **"Different" isn't a value statement, so avoid being judgmental.**

Find One, Be One

God made us for connections. We are the living, breathing body of Christ, not an amalgamation of marbles that bounce off each other. We can only be the people He wants us to be and achieve the dream He has planned for us if we are surrounded by trusted friends and mentors. Do you have someone like that? If you do, I'm sure you treasure that person (or people), but if not, don't stop looking. Not everyone believes God has something special for each of us, and some think that wealth and power are the true measure of a dream. Keep looking until you find someone with clear eyes and a humble heart, someone who can see beyond the surface and speak truth to your soul. Those people are out there. Don't quit looking until you find them.

But real fulfillment comes when we take on the mantle of being dream releasers for other people. I love the thrill of God using me in that way. There's tremendous power in the spoken word when it comes from the heart. Pastor Robert Lewis says there are three messages every child needs to hear often from parents: "I love you," "I'm proud of you," and "You're good at this or that."[3] Spouses need to hear those messages, too. I think of difficult times my girls went through when I was led to tell them: "I understand how you're feeling, and I want to assure you that God has something wonderful for you. You may not see it now, but it'll come. I can promise you that God is working out good things even when you can't see them." In times of heartache and discouragement, we can be there for those we love. We may not have all the answers. In fact, if we come across as having all the answers, we lower our credibility. Sometimes, we have to simply say, "I'm here, and I care." We may not know what God is up to, but we can be sure it's always good and right. As the English pastor Charles Spurgeon said, "God is too good to be unkind.

He is too wise to be confused. If I cannot trace his hand, I can always trust his heart."[4]

In our relationships with some people, God uses us to *release* their dreams, but in the lives of others, He uses us to *restore* broken dreams. Many people who have lost hope in their dreams sit next to us in church each week and interact with us every day in our businesses. They're living quiet lives of desperation—without hope, without passion, and without meaningful connections. Their goal each day is just to survive. The message of the Bible is that God is never through with us. In fact, He delights in changing the trajectory of the lives of broken, discarded people. No one is beyond the grace of God to save or below the hope of being used by God to accomplish something wonderful. When we find broken, wounded, discouraged people, we can assure them that God isn't finished with them. The stories in the Bible—from the schemer Jacob to the adulterer David to the betrayer Peter and countless others—give us strong hope that God is reaching out His kind, strong hand, waiting for the outcasts to take it again.

The Roofers

Once, when Jesus was on His home turf in the region of Capernaum and spoke to a group at a house, the curious crowd grew so large that people were spilling out into the yard. Four friends heard that "the miracle worker" was in town, and they wanted to take their paralyzed buddy to Jesus. They picked him up and carried him to the house, but when they arrived, they couldn't get in. I can imagine them looking in every door and window to see if they could get their friend in front of Jesus. Then one of them probably pointed to the roof, and they all clamored up there, lugging their buddy on their backs. Mark picks up the story:

"Some men came, bringing to him a paralyzed man, carried by four of them. Since they could not get him to Jesus because of the crowd, they made an opening in the roof above Jesus by digging through it and then lowered the mat the man was lying on" (Mark 2:3,4).

Can you imagine the scene inside the house? Jesus was speaking about the kingdom of God, telling stories and helping people understand who He was. Then, the crowd began hearing some noise up at the ceiling. In a few minutes, some plaster began falling all around Jesus. After a few minutes, a little hole appeared, and then it got bigger. A head popped down into the room to make sure their calculations were right. After the man's head disappeared, more hands got to work, and big chunks of ceiling and roof fell to the floor. I would imagine Jesus was covered in dust. Now the opening was large—large enough for a pallet to be lowered right in front of Jesus. I can almost see the smile on His face and hear His laugh. "When Jesus saw their faith, he said to the paralyzed man, 'Son, your sins are forgiven'" (verse 6).

Notice that Mark didn't say, "When Jesus saw the *paralyzed man's* faith," but "When Jesus saw *their* faith"—the faith of the roofers. Because of their faith, Jesus performed two miracles. He forgave the paralyzed man's sins, meeting his ultimate spiritual need, and then He healed his paralysis, meeting his physical need.

The roofers aren't named in Mark's story, but what they did has been told for generations. They didn't have supernatural power, but they released a friend's dream of being forgiven and healed. In the same way, many of the people who made a big difference in my life aren't celebrities. They're just ordinary people who were willing for God to use them in extraordinary ways.

And of course, Jesus is the ultimate dream releaser. He welcomes the broken and discarded, and He brings them into the light of hope. In

Him, they are more valuable than the stars in the sky. He welcomes the proud and judgmental, and His grace humbles them to the dust. Then He raises them with a new heart and a new purpose to honor Him with all their hearts. No one is outside of God's incredible dream. Without Jesus, we're just playing games to impress and control. But when He infuses our lives with love and purpose, we become His partners in the great adventure.

Changing the Culture

The laws of nature and human nature tell us that systems don't improve unless injected with something positive. In other words, a family, a small group, a church, a business, or any collection of people in any organization doesn't become a dynamic group of dream releasers until someone takes the initiative to make it happen. All it takes is one dream releaser to change everything.

Many times, I've talked to Gail and told her about my doubts, or I've told my small group of friends that I'm struggling and want to quit, or I've been honest with a mentor about my sense of inadequacy, and these dear people have spoken words of faith, hope, and love back into my heart. They are the roofers in my life. When I was paralyzed by fear and doubt, they picked me up, dug through the roof of my complaints, and lowered me to the feet of Jesus. Quite often, their efforts took some time to break through the crust and get to the heart, but then, the roofers had to do plenty of labor to show their love, too.

During the death part of the cycle of a dream, people desperately need someone to come along to give them a hug, share a word of hope, and give assurance that the dream isn't over. In fact, a resurrection is coming. The death phase is the time when most people give up, so dream releasers need to be especially vigilant and intentional during that time. When people become discouraged, they tend to withdraw or lash out in anger. We need to notice them, move toward them, look past their protests that "nothing's wrong," or conversely, that "the world is going to end," and inject a new word of hope into their lives.

Let me make some suggestions about how to change the culture of any group of people. Like the roofers, look beneath the surface to find meaning and hope. With people, look past their surface demeanor and into their hearts. On the outside, they may look intimidating or piti-ful, passive or controlling, but these are often defense mechanisms to keep people from noticing hidden hurt, fear, and resentment. Dream releasers know that what's on the outside is often a disguise. They know better than to react to only what they see and hear. When the time is right, they ask questions and explore the person's heart. And dream releasers are more excited about others' success than their own. In fact, like Dr. McGee, they celebrate whenever family members, friends, or co-workers take a bold step toward their dream—even if the attempt is less than success-ful. They applaud the character quality of courage and the willingness to try something new.

Dream releasers are more excited about others' success than their own.

To make that kind of mark in people's lives, especially in the lives of young people today, we need to accept, believe, and challenge. We accept them for who they are. They may come from a different part of town or a different country. They may have tattoos or body piercings. But we look past all that into their hearts. Like Jesus with the woman at the well, we see the person and not all the baggage she carries (John 4:1–38). What does it mean to accept someone? I think it means that we don't criticize, correct, or harp on things that don't matter to Jesus. And we care deeply about the things that thrilled Him or broke His heart. We're sure—even if they're not certain—that God hasn't given up on them. We take time to uncover their desires and hidden talents. And we don't sit back and let them rust. We challenge them to ask God for opportunities to try out their talents and see what happens. Sometimes they thrive, and sometimes they fail. Either way, they still need our words of kindness and hope that God is doing a wonderful thing in their lives.

Every culture—family, church, neighborhood, and business—has strengths and weaknesses. In some ways, we'd think church would be the easiest place to be a dream releaser, but some church people can be incredibly narrow, harsh, and condemning. They delight in pointing out faults, but they aren't willing to step into a person's life to help them take a step forward. In business, we may expect people to be cutthroat, but I've found some of the most genuine faith and love in business environments. In companies around the country, men and women live out their faith every day with integrity and care for those around them. Families can be the most powerfully positive environment on the planet, or they can be a source of confusion and heartache. But every culture can be transformed into something beautiful. It only takes one husband or wife or child or friend or co-worker to make a difference. It only takes a single roofer to care less about his reputation and more about helping someone in need. It only takes one person to look beyond a teenager's anger to touch her heart. It only takes one manager who is genuinely thrilled when an employee succeeds.

I want to make my mark as a dream releaser in the lives of those around me. I'm pretty sure there won't be any statues of me or buildings named after me when I'm gone, but I hope some people think of me, smile, and say, "Yeah, Doug believed in me when no one else did, and it made all the difference in the world."

Do you want to be a dream releaser, too?

What's Your Take?

1. How would you define and describe a "dream releaser"?

2. As you grew up, who were some dream releasers in your life? What difference have they made? How would your life be different if they hadn't come along at the right time?

3. Why is it important to understand the differences between how men and women process information and emotions? How might these insights help you in an important relationship or two?

4. Who is a dream releaser in your life today?

5. In whose life are you playing that role (or do you feel led to play that role)?

6. What do you think motivated the four friends in Mark's story? How do you think these people felt and responded to their faith: Jesus, the paralyzed man, and the people in the house?

7. Think about the culture of your family, school, work, neighborhood, and church. What are some specific things you can do to change the culture by accepting people, believing in them, and challenging them to find and follow God's dream?

Prayer of Commitment

Jesus, thank You for being the ultimate dream releaser. You noticed me when I had nothing to offer, and You gave me love, purpose and hope. Use me, Lord. Open my eyes to see the needs in people around me, and give me courage to use the resources of my life to release their dreams. Amen.

7 Keeping the Dream from Fading

Our Adversary majors in three things: noise, hurry and crowds. If he can

keep us engaged in "muchness" and "manyness," he will rest satisfied.

—Richard J. Foster

Everybody can come up with excuses to abandon their dream. Courageous people, though, find a way to keep going. Ben Comen is one of those people. Ben is the slowest cross-country runner in the nation. In fact, he owns the record for the worst time in an event. His goal in each race is to beat his personal best time of 40 minutes for a 3.1-mile race. Ben was born with cerebral palsy. Since birth, he has suffered from debilitating muscle control. Running is quite a task for him, but he loves it. He explains, "I'm more relaxed when I run. When I run, nothing bothers me much."

As is the case with many disabled kids who long to play sports, most coaches were willing for Ben to be a water boy or sit on the bench. No one thought he could actually compete. His parents signed him up for every sport in school, but all the coaches turned him down. Finally, Chuck Parker agreed to include Ben on the eighth-grade cross-country team.

Ben threw himself into training. He knew he would never cross the finish line first, but his joy in running drove him to get up every morning and run around the town of Anderson, South Carolina. His siblings went with him some days, but most of the time he ran alone.

In races in high school, Ben stood at the starting line with all the other competitors. After the starting gun sounded, they all left him in their tracks. They vanished over the hills, but Ben never quit. Even when he fell, which was often, he got up and kept going. His example inspired those watching and those who were running. In many races, participants who finished well ahead of him looped back and joined him to run to the finish line. They wanted to "run him home." At the finish, it looked like Ben was the victor in the Boston Marathon. As he and his entourage neared the finish, the crowd cheered wildly. A commentator noted, "Ben Comen's inspirational story is a humbling one to us all. If someone with cerebral palsy could have a dream and fulfill it, what more is called of those of us who are normal. Ben Comen has been running all his life. Not from something but towards something."[1]

Shattered or Eroded

Our dreams can be shattered in a moment by a colossal failure, sin, or tragedy. Sexual or moral sin produces a nagging, haunting sense of shame. Many people who sin this way feel their lives are over. They secretly wonder, "How could God ever use someone as flawed as me. I'm history." The shattering of a dream sometimes is the result of another person's sin. Those who suffer from abuse, abandonment, or violence feel traumatized. To try to cope with the pain, they become passive or driven, isolated or clinging to others. Like an accident victim who can only think about his broken leg, these people have difficulty looking outside themselves. To them, it would be a dream just to make it through another day.

Far more people, though, struggle with a gradual erosion of their dreams. They start strong, with passion and energy to be the person God wants them to be and to do what He has called them to do. But the steady drip of discouragement, negative messages, lack of appreciation, and exhaustion causes their dream to fade. After a while, they remember the dream wistfully, "Yeah, I used to be excited about what God was doing in my life, but that was a long time ago."

Every dream endures seasons of atrophy and entropy. Like a withered arm, the strength of a dream can fade if we aren't around people who continually believe in us, reinforce our passion, and gently correct us when we get off track. And some of us experience entropy, a randomness caused by too many distractions and competing goals. Instead of staying on task, we flit from one good idea to another, never quite finishing a task before we jump into something else. This can be exciting, but it's also exhausting—for us and for those around us.

To keep God's dream from fading, we need to understand that God is always at work behind the scenes. Even when we don't see it, we can be sure that He is accomplishing His divine purposes—if we'll just hang on and trust Him in the darkness.

Joseph's Dream

The story of the patriarchs is checkered with tragic sin and glowing faith. Through Abraham, Isaac, and Jacob, we see God using terribly flawed people to fulfill His goal of blessing the entire world. By the fourth generation, the family includes twelve sons, including Joseph, Jacob's favorite. In every generation, parents had shown preference of one child over another, and it always caused tremendous heartache. Joseph's beautiful mother Rachel had died giving birth to his brother Benjamin. Jacob doted on his favorite child, giving him more honor than his brothers, including a beautiful, multi-colored robe—and they hated him for it. When Joseph was seventeen, God gave him two dreams (Genesis 37:1–11). In his first dream, his brothers bowed down to him. Telling his brothers this dream may not have been the most diplomatic move in the young man's life. His brothers barked, "Do you intend to reign over us? Will you actually rule us?" (Genesis 37:8) And they despised him even more. In his second dream, his whole family, including his father, bowed down to him. In an ancient patriarchal family, this was unthinkable! This time, even his father was upset with him.

To show how little Joseph and his father grasped the strife in the family, Jacob sent Joseph out to the fields to check up on his brothers. When Joseph arrived at their camp many miles away from home, they realized they had an opportunity to get rid of him. "'Here comes that dreamer!' they said to each other. 'Come now, let's kill him and throw him into one of these cisterns and say that a ferocious animal devoured him. Then we'll see what comes of his dreams'" (Genesis 37:19,20). They planned to kill him, but one of the brothers, Reuben, wanted to rescue the boy and take him back to their father. They threw Joseph in a well, and they ripped his coat and put blood on it to show their dad and claim a wild animal had killed him. However, before Reuben could get back and get Joseph out, the other brothers sold him to a caravan headed to Egypt. The dream seemed to fade, but God wasn't finished with Joseph.

In Egypt, a wealthy official named Potiphar bought Joseph and made him his household slave. The young man proved to be a capable administrator, so Potiphar put him in charge of all his possessions. In the young slave's hands, the household thrived. Potiphar's wife was attracted to the handsome young Jew, and she asked him to go to bed with her. When he ran away, she tore his cloak and told Potiphar that Joseph had tried to rape her. I don't think Potiphar believed his wife, or he would have had Joseph executed. Instead, he had him thrown into prison, where he languished for perhaps twenty years (Genesis 39:1–20).

In the prison, the warden realized this young man was an extraordinary prisoner. He put him in charge of the prison, and again, Joseph flourished (Genesis 39:21–23)—but the dream must have seemed a long way away. After many years, two members of Pharaoh's household staff were thrown into prison. Both of them had disturbing dreams. They turned to Joseph to interpret them: he had good news and bad news. He told the cupbearer that he would be restored to his position of honor and service, but the baker would be condemned to death. In three days, both of these predictions proved true (Genesis 40:1–23).

I can imagine that Joseph's hopes were sky high at that point. He had remained faithful to the Lord during the most grueling, senseless suffering he could imagine. "Now," I'm sure he thought, "the cupbearer will put in a good word for me with the pharaoh, and he'll let me out of here." It wasn't to be. The cupbearer promptly forgot about Joseph, so he continued to languish in prison.

Some time later, Pharaoh had two disturbing dreams. His magicians and wise men couldn't interpret them. Then the cupbearer remembered Joseph and explained to Pharaoh about the prisoner who had accurately interpreted two dreams. Pharaoh sent for Joseph at once. Joseph washed and put on clean clothes. When he appeared at court, Pharaoh told him his two dreams. Joseph explained that the first one foretold seven years of good harvest, but the second predicted seven years of famine. But

Joseph wasn't finished. He advised the most powerful man in the world to find a capable administrator who could oversee the gathering and storing of surplus grain during the good years so there would be enough food during the famine. Pharaoh picked Joseph—the abandoned, forsaken, despised, and forgotten prisoner—to be his new prime minister (Genesis 41:1–40)

For seven years, Joseph made sure plenty of grain was stored. Then, when famine hit the whole region, the Egyptians had plenty of food. Another family, however, was running short of supplies. Jacob, his sons, and their families were starving. They heard there was food in Egypt, so Jacob sent ten of his sons (all except Benjamin, his youngest) to Egypt to buy food (Genesis 42:1–8). When they arrived, they had no idea that the person in command of the empire was their brother. When they met him, they didn't recognize him. Through a series of events, Joseph tested his brothers to see if they had changed since they betrayed him two decades earlier (Genesis 42:14–17, 44:1–34). Finally, they passed the tests, and he was convinced they had changed. It was time to tell them who he really was.

Then Joseph could no longer control himself before all his attendants, and he cried out, "Have everyone leave my presence!" So there was no one with Joseph when he made himself known to his brothers. And he wept so loudly that the Egyptians heard him, and Pharaoh's household heard about it.

Joseph said to his brothers, "I am Joseph! Is my father still living?" But his brothers were not able to answer him, because they were terrified at his presence (Genesis 45:1–3).

I'm not sure when things clicked for Joseph, but at some point, he realized that all the twists and turns of the plot of his dream finally made sense. All those years as a slave, in prison, and as prime minister of the most powerful nation on earth were part of God's divine plan to rescue his family from famine and starvation. Each roadblock was a stepping stone to fulfill God's dream. And those dreams he had when he was a boy? They came true as his father and brothers honored him when they came to Egypt to live at the pharaoh's invitation.

When Jacob died, the brothers were afraid Joseph would take the opportunity to exact revenge. In response to their fear, Joseph assured them, "Don't be afraid. Am I in the place of God? You intended to harm me, but God intended it for good to accomplish what is now being done, the saving of many lives. So then, don't be afraid. I will provide for you and your children" (Genesis 50:19–21).

Joseph's story of tenacious faith is one of the most challenging and inspiring in the Bible—or in any literature. At a thousand points, his dream could have faded to black. He endured the worst of heartaches and betrayals, and he had to do what people instinctively hate to do: wait on an answer. Through all those years, he didn't wallow in self-pity and resentment. When God finally opened the door for Joseph to be ushered into Pharaoh's throne room, he was ready. He was spiritually, mentally, and physically prepared to fulfill the dream God had given him many years before. Nothing could stop him. Nothing.

> **Through all those years, he didn't wallow in self-pity and resentment. When God finally opened the door for Joseph to be ushered into Pharaoh's throne room, he was ready.**

R³

Joseph was a victim of unfair circumstances—genuine injustice. As we follow God's dream for our lives, we are foolish if we think it will go smoothly. We'll experience our fair share of ugly situations and searing accusations. We may be passed over for a job, ignored by someone we love, suffer from accidents or illness, or experience countless other setbacks. Our response depends on our perspective. Our circumstances aren't a surprise to God. He knows, He cares, and He's creative and powerful enough to weave everything—even our sins and the sins of others—into the fabric of a glorious future. To stay strong, we need to live by three Rs: remember, return, and repeat.

Remember

My dream tends to fade when I'm tired, when I don't feel appreciated, when my ideas aren't accepted, and when I believe I'm overlooked. When I'm exhausted, I lose focus when I hear glowing stories of the successes of other leaders. At those times, I wonder, "But what about me? Doesn't anybody notice what I'm doing for God?"

In all those years in slavery and in prison—and even when he was in a position of power in Egypt—Joseph surely thought about the two dreams he had when he was a young man. He may not have understood their implications, but he knew they came from God, and God would be faithful to accomplish them. During times of darkness, dismay, and discouragement, Joseph remembered God's dream for his life.

Today, we have far more information about the nature of God and His promises. We have the entire Bible to remind us of God's grace, His purposes, and the complexity of His plan for His people. When I feel my heart drifting and the dream begins to fade, I need to remember that Almighty God has called me to be His child. I belong to Him. He has the right to determine my path. I may feel entitled to a smooth, easy life—until I remember that the One I call Savior suffered at the hands of evil people to rescue me from sin and death. When I remember Jesus' love for me, I can live with open-handed, full-hearted devotion to Him. Everything I am and everything I have is a gift from Him. I deserve nothing, but I've received everything. A few minutes of reflection can get me back on track with faith and thankfulness. Even when I don't see the light at the end of the tunnel, I remember Joseph's tenacious faith in God's dream—and I can take another step toward God and His dream for me.

One of the things Joseph had to remember all those years was that the price he was paying would be worth the dream. He didn't know what the ultimate meaning of his suffering might be, but he was sure that God "rewards those who earnestly seek him" (Hebrews 11:6). He was a handsome young man when he was in Potiphar's house. He had been betrayed and abandoned by his brothers, and he could easily have justified falling into the arms of a woman who wanted him. He paid a steep price to say no to her. He also paid a price to remain cheerful and faith-filled when he spent those long years in prison. He had no idea what God was up to, but he remembered the dreams and stayed strong.

I don't want to give the impression that if we aren't as faithful as Joseph we'll miss our dream. Far from it! The Scriptures are full of stories of people who committed sins, made dumb choices, and failed in many different ways, but God didn't give up on them. We remember the incredible grace of God to restore us, just as we remember the dream He wants us to follow.

Return

At any given point of the day or night, thousands of airplanes fly across the country. Pilots file a flight plan before takeoff, but once in the air, the jet stream, storms, and other winds push them off course. As they fly, pilots make continuous course corrections to get back on the original path. They don't return to the path just once; they do so throughout the entire flight.

Spiritually, we often have to return to the Lord and be refreshed. In the letters to the seven churches in Revelation, John records Jesus' message to each of them. Speaking to the church in Ephesus,, Jesus commended believers there for their hard work, spiritual perception, and endurance. Then he gave them a word of correction: "Yet I hold this against you: You have forsaken the love you had at first. Consider how far you have fallen! Repent and do the things you did at first. If you do not repent, I will come to you and remove your lampstand from its place" (Revelation 2:4,5). The Lord was saying, "You've drifted. Come back. Return to me and I'll restore you." In fact, if they responded, Jesus gave them this promise: "To the one who is victorious, I will give the right to eat from the tree of life, which is in the paradise of God" (verse 7).

In our lives, we're sometimes surprised when a passage of Scripture or a trusted friend points out that we've drifted from the trajectory of our dream. A nagging and destructive habit, a bad attitude, laziness, or strained relationships signal that we're off track—maybe just a little, or maybe a lot. For believers, course corrections need to be SOP, "standard operating procedure." In fact, when Martin Luther began the Reformation in 1517 by nailing his "95 Theses" to the door of the church at Wittenberg, the first one stated, "When our Lord and Master, Jesus Christ, said 'Repent,' He called for the entire life of believers to be one of repentance."[2] The "entire life of believers"—not once in a blue moon, not when we can't avoid it any longer, but all day every day as the Spirit of God whispers, "Turn this way," "Say this to that person," "Forgive instead of harboring a grudge," "Don't say a word," "Tell the truth no matter what," and a thousand other corrections. As we let our minds feast on God's Word and walk in the Spirit, we make as many corrections in our daily lives as a pilot makes on a cross-country flight.

Repeat

Joseph didn't waste his days in anger and blame. Undoubtedly, he rehearsed the dreams of his youth many times to make sure his heart stayed fixed on God. Scripture repeats certain themes again and again, as if the Lord thinks we're so dense that we won't get it the first time. Unfortunately, He's right. repeat over and over. For example, in the Old Testament, God instructed the children of Israel through Moses to repeat a description of His nature and His purposes for them every day:

Hear, O Israel: The LORD our God, the LORD is one._Love the LORD your God with all your heart and with all your soul and with all your strength. These commandments that I give you today are to be on your hearts. Impress them on your children. Talk about them when you sit at home and when you walk along the road, when you lie down and when you get up. Tie them as symbols on your hands and bind them on your foreheads. Write them on the doorframes of your houses and on your gates (Deuteronomy 6:5–9).

When were they to repeat God's truth? All day, every day. Where? Every place they went each day. Like Israel, we need to repeat God's truth every day until it's written on our hearts.

Waiting

Like most people, I hate to wait. We've been conditioned to expect instant answers to questions and solutions to our problems. When we have to wait more than a few minutes in a line, we go crazy. The need for speed is, to some degree, part of the human condition, but our culture puts this expectation on steroids. When we read the Scriptures, we see God's incredible patience in accomplishing His purposes. We see the cycles of seasons in farming. For long periods of time, God seems to be silent before He bursts on the scene. We might be in a hurry, but He's not. Solomon said, "[God] has made everything beautiful in its time" (Ecclesiastes 3:11). Paul tells us that Jesus came in "the fullness of time" (Galatians 4:4, KJV), but He appeared more than four hundred years after Malachi prophesied His coming (Malachi 4:5). For all those generations, people had the promise but not the Person.

Joseph waited in darkness for twenty years. It's unreasonable to think that we won't have to wait for the fulfillment of our dream, too. During those long weeks, months, and years, the dream can fade; or, if we dig deep into the heart of God, the dream can grow stronger. How sure are we that God will come through on His promises? The Psalmist compared our wait with a soldier who stands watch over the city at night. All night, the soldier keeps his eyes peeled, looking for any enemy that might sneak up on the city. When morning comes and the light shines, the danger of a sneak attack is over. The Psalmist wrote:

I wait for the LORD, my whole being waits,
and in his word I put my hope.
I wait for the Lord
more than watchmen wait for the morning,
more than watchmen wait for the morning (Psalm 130:5,6).

Waiting on the Lord doesn't mean we sit passively until He shows up. Waiting isn't really about time; it's about expectation. We long for God to move, we trust He'll show up at the right time, and as we wait, we continue to serve in the work He has called us to do.

I believe that when Joseph looked back at his life as an old man, he was satisfied with God's path for his dream, and he wouldn't change a thing. In the middle of the disappointments and delays, he wondered what God was up to, but he never let the dream fade. He kept trusting, kept clinging, and kept believing that God

Waiting isn't really about time; it's about expectation.

would someday, somehow make the dream come true. He had a tenacious faith in God's sovereignty. Faith kept him going when times got tough. He didn't understand God's plan until he looked in the rearview mirror, but he trusted God anyway.

Joseph's dream produced a sustainable hope and a lasting conviction. Such hope promises a good ending to the story, no matter what's going on in the middle chapters. In our lives, too, we can't predict when the last chapter will be written or what the details of the ending will be, but we trust in a good, sovereign, and powerful God who holds all things in His hands.

I love to hear stories of people who continue trusting God when their dreams seem to be shattered. Former NBC news anchor Tom Brokaw interviewed the wife of a young soldier who had been crippled by an enemy shell. Her husband had severe brain damage and impaired motor skills. She held up a picture of the two of them taken the day before his deployment. She sighed, "This is what we had." Then she looked over at her husband in his wheelchair and smiled, "But this is what we have now, and we're determined to find real happiness in this reality."

There's a tension between the ideal and the real. If we insist on the ideal, we'll complain, blame, and miss the blessings of God. But if we embrace reality and trust God to work in it, we can rest assured that God will move in powerful ways. A single mom may have the dream of providing a quality education for her children. Money may be tight, but she's willing to work two jobs to earn enough to get them into the right. A college student may have a dream of going to law school or into medicine, but her board scores aren't quite good enough. Instead of giving up, she studies hard and tries again. A couple may have struggled for years in their marriage. They've thought many times about getting a divorce, but they have a tenacious hope that God can work in each of their hearts to overcome the barriers and build bridges of love and trust. An older man with a terminal illness prays for healing, but is content also to pray, "Not my will, but Thy will." Whether God heals him or not, he's determined to be the most loving, positive grandfather his grandchildren can have. A person who has been out of work for months may feel like giving up, but she keeps turning over stones, looking for retraining opportunities, and trusting that God will provide. The examples of sustainable hope and lasting conviction are endless. Every dream is different, and God's unique plan for each person is expertly crafted. We can look to others for inspiration, but we shouldn't look at God's path for them as the exact model of what He wants to do in our lives. God had a specialized dream for Joseph, Elijah, Mary, Paul, and the other people we've met in the Bible. But he also has a specialized dream for us, which we must find and follow.   In the inevitable delays and discouragement, we aren't passive. We feed our faith and starve our doubts. We need an arsenal of truth and encouragement from God's word. Jeremiah had it right when he wrote:

When your words came, I ate them;
they were my joy and my heart's delight,
for I bear your name,
LORD God Almighty (Jeremiah 15:16).

We "eat" God's word the same way we eat tangible food: we search for pertinent passage or theme in the Bible, prepare it by studying, chew it by meditating on it, and then let it nourish our hearts.

The Ultimate Hope

We'd like to have ironclad guarantees in this life that God will make us happy, wealthy, healthy, and thin, but life doesn't work that way. People lose their jobs, their health, and their hair. Sometimes, we can take action to arrest this process of loss, but sooner or later, we succumb. What is our ultimate hope? What can we count on from God? I know a young mother who has been diagnosed with cirrhosis of the liver. She has received the finest medical care on the planet. At times, she hoped things would turn out just fine or that her condition would be treatable with medicine. Recently, however, when she met with a specialist, she didn't hear good news. The cirrhosis has advanced to a stage where she needs a liver transplant. When this young woman called her parents to give them the update, her news devastated them. But she comforted them: "We're trusting God for healing, but no matter what happens, we believe God is allowing us to go through this process in some way for our good, our children's good, and for His glory. We trust in Him!" Talk about faith and hope!

At one point in his suffering, Paul said he longed to leave this earth and go to be with Christ (Philippians 1:23,24). In his second letter to the

Corinthians, he described his bedrock faith in God's ultimate goal of restoring all creation in the new heaven and new earth. Until then, we wait, but we wait with eager anticipation of a glorious future. Paul explained how to respond to suffering today:

> Therefore we do not lose heart. Though outwardly we are wasting away, yet inwardly we are being renewed day by day. For our light and momentary troubles are achieving for us an eternal glory that far outweighs them all. So we fix our eyes not on what is seen, but on what is unseen, since what is seen is temporary, but what is unseen is eternal (2 Corinthians 4:16–18).

Our physical eyes can't see a future that is beyond anything we can imagine, but our spiritual eyes can. In his sermon "The Weight of Glory," C. S. Lewis says that in the new heaven and new earth, five things will be true: we'll be with Christ, we'll be transformed to be like Him, we'll enjoy a magnificent feast with the family of God, we'll enjoy the glory of God's affirmation ("Well done!"), and we'll have a role to reign with Christ forever.[3]

How do we keep the dream from fading? By focusing our eyes away from our struggles and onto Christ's goodness and greatness. As we think about being with Him forever, we'll realize that everything we do in this life really matters—especially our faith in God during tough times.

What's Your Take?

1. What are some ways dreams are shattered? How are they eroded?

2. What do you think kept Joseph strong during all those years in slavery and prison? How can you apply those principles?

3. Describe why it's important to develop the habits of "remember, return, and repeat" to stay on track with your dream?

4. How well do you wait? What are some of God's purposes for causing us to wait?

5. While we wait, what's our responsibility? What's God's responsibility?

6. What are some practical ways you can feed your faith and starve your doubts?

7. Why is it important to think deeply and often about our ultimate hope of the new heaven and new earth?

Prayer of Commitment

Jesus, You never let the dream fade, even though You endured ridicule, misunderstanding, and heartache. Thank You for the example of Joseph. His tenacious faith and forgiveness points me toward You. Give me courage, Lord, to face the things that cause me to drift, and help me remember, return, and repeat Your promises often. Amen.

8 Scripting Your Dream

My Prayer for Each of You: that you would have a rich life of Joy and Power, abundant in Supernatural results, with a constant, clear vision of never-ending life in God's World before you, and of the everlasting significance of your work day by day. A radiant life and death.

—Dallas Willard

Screenwriting and playwriting appear to be the same skill, but there's a profound difference. When screenwriters produce dialogue and descriptions of action for a movie, they know the director can do retakes until he gets the scene right. Some directors shoot a particular scene one hundred times! After all these takes, the editor works his magic to carefully craft each second of the film. When we go to the theater, we can be sure that every moment is exactly what the writer and director want it to be. Playwrights carefully craft each scene, too, but the production venue is different from a movie. There's one take, and it's live. If an actor speaks a line at the wrong time or moves to the wrong place, the rest of the cast must adapt on the fly. Some actors love the spontaneity of the stage, but others feel uncomfortable with the immediacy and flexibility required of a stage performance. As we plan the story of our dreams, we are like those who write plays. We think carefully about how the action and dialogue should go, but we're aware that we'll have to make adjustments on the fly.

Planning and Spontaneity

Our dreams don't just happen. They result from brainstorming, planning, and implementation. Bishop N. T. Wright observes that many Christians today belong to "the cult of spontaneity," believing that planning is somehow counter-Christian. Such a belief is foreign to Scripture. God carefully planned our salvation "before the foundation of the world" (Ephesians 1:4, ESV). Jesus went to the cross according to "God's deliberate plan and foreknowledge" (Acts 2:23). Paul planned his missionary journeys to particular cities; the pattern of his efforts took him first to the synagogues and then to the streets to tell people about Jesus . These examples show that planning is essential. As we contemplate the dream God has put on our hearts, we experience the joy of being a creative playwright and the responsibility of adapting to every new instruction of the Heavenly Director.

Sometimes, things don't go the way we planned. Brian Hice had a day like that in Provo, Utah.[1] First, a pipe in the apartment above his broke, flooding his apartment, so the apartment manager told him to rent a water vacuum. As he left to drive to the store, he noticed he had a flat tire. He went back inside to phone a friend for help. He had to stand in water to pick up the phone. An electrical shock jolted him, and his violent reflex ripped the phone off the wall. After a few minutes, he gathered himself and prepared to leave, but water damage had swelled his door jamb shut. He yelled for a neighbor to come and kick the door down. While all this was happening, somebody stole Brian's car. However, because it was almost out of gas, Brian found it a few blocks away. He pushed it to a gas station to fill it up.

That evening, Brian planned to attend a military ceremony at his university. When he got in his car, however, he severely injured himself when he sat on a bayonet he had carelessly tossed on the front seat. Doctors stitched his wound that night, but no one could resuscitate Brian's four canaries, who were crushed by fallen plaster from his wet apartment ceiling.

When Brian finally returned home after a long night at the hospital, he slipped on the wet floor and injured his tailbone. Later, he told a friend, "God wanted me dead, but he just kept missing."

Brian Hice had to rewrite his story all day. We are both writers and actors in our own plays, which we continue to rewrite every day as we adapt to the changes our Director gives us. To make the most of our story, we have to listen well and write creatively. We can learn great lessons about adaptivity from people in the Bible. I want to draw some principles from the life of one of those people: King Jehoshaphat.

An Unusual Battle Strategy

The story of the kings after David and Solomon is a long, sad tale, punctuated with moments of glory. King Asa was a faithless king. To appease an enemy ruler, he took gold and silver out of God's temple to use as a payoff. After he died a painful, lonely death, his son Jehoshaphat became king. This man, though, trusted God, and God honored him with power and wealth. An able administrator and planner, the new king appointed judges throughout the land. He instructed them:

Consider carefully what you do, because you are not judging for mere mortals but for the LORD, who is with you whenever you give a verdict. Now let the fear of the LORD be on you. Judge carefully, for

with the LORD our God there is no injustice or partiality or bribery
(2 Chronicles 19:6,7).

Some may think that faith and obedience guarantee blessing, but they don't. Although Jehoshaphat led his people with courage and pointed them to God, an armed alliance of Moabites, Ammonites, and Meunites invaded his landLORD, and he proclaimed a fast for all Judah. The people of Judah came together to seek help from the LORD; indeed, they came from every town in Judah to seek him" (2 Chronicles 20:3,4).

But the king didn't panic. The narrator tells us, "Alarmed, Jehoshaphat resolved to inquire of the Jehoshaphat didn't respond to the crisis by running around trying to figure out what to do. First, he prayed—not just a quick "Help me!" prayer, either, but an intense prayer of intercession by him and everyone else in his kingdom. Jehoshaphat didn't consider prayer something to tack on at the end of planning. He considered it essential to getting God's perspective.

As he met with the others and they sought the God together, he prayed, "LORD, the God of our ancestors, are you not the God who is in heaven? You rule over all the kingdoms of the nations. Power and might are in your hand, and no one can withstand you" (verse 6). He didn't begin his prayer with a list of petitions. He started by declaring the majesty of God. When we pray, we remember passages of Scripture that proclaim the goodness, greatness, wisdom, love, and sovereignty of God. Near the end of Paul's explanation of God's plan of salvation for the nations, he stopped and exploded in praise:

Oh, the depth of the riches of the wisdom and knowledge of God!
How unsearchable his judgments,

and his paths beyond tracing out!
"Who has known the mind of the Lord?
Or who has been his counselor?'
"Who has ever given to God,
that God should repay them?"
For from him and through him and for him are all things.
To him be the glory forever! Amen (Romans 11:33–36).

Then the king recounted God's promises and past deliverance for His people. He's reminding God, himself and those listening to him that nothing is too hard for God. He prayed:

Our God, did you not drive out the inhabitants of this land before your people Israel and give it forever to the descendants of Abraham your friend? They have lived in it and have built in it a sanctuary for your Name, saying, "If calamity comes upon us, whether the sword of judgment, or plague or famine, we will stand in your presence before this temple that bears your Name and will cry out to you in our distress, and you will hear us and save us" (verses 7–9).

As we think about what's going on in our lives, we can reflect on God's work in the past: a broken marriage restored, a prodigal come home, the healing of someone who was sick, God's gracious presence in times of grief, a new job when finances were tight, the salvation of someone we love, and dozens of other memories of God's faithfulness and power. This exercise isn't just for fun. It's a discipline that strengthens our faith at a time when it may waver. God's past faithfulness reminds us of God's blessings in our history and predicts future blessing.

Only then did Jehoshaphat offer his request to God. His prayer wasn't general and mushy. It was urgent and specific. He didn't minimize the danger, and he didn't ignore reality. He was completely honest about the risk because his heart had grown stronger by his praise and memories. He pointedly asked God:

> But now here are men from Ammon, Moab and Mount Seir, whose territory you would not allow Israel to invade when they came from Egypt; so they turned away from them and did not destroy them. See how they are repaying us by coming to drive us out of the possession you gave us as an inheritance. Our God, will you not judge them? For we have no power to face this vast army that is attacking us. We do not know what to do, but our eyes are on you (verses 10–12).

The king was well aware of the problem, but his eyes focused on the greatness of God, not the power of the armies allied against him. Corrie ten Boom knew something of stress and heartache. She and her sister Betsy endured Nazi concentration camps during World War II. Betsy died, but Corrie lived through the ordeal. Every day of hunger, lice, bitter cold, hard labor, abuse, and the prospect of death, Corrie learned to lean heavily on the Lord. Later, she commented, "If you look at the world, you'll be distressed. If you look within you, you'll be depressed. If you look at Christ, you'll be at rest."[2]

At that point, the Spirit spoke through a prophet to the king and his people. He told them, "Listen, King Jehoshaphat and all who live in Judah and Jerusalem! This is what the LORD says to you: 'Do not be afraid or discouraged because of this vast army. For the battle is not yours, but God's'" (verse 15). When the king and his people heard this word, they bowed down and worshipped the Lord.

The king's battle strategy was odd. He appointed a choir to sing as they marched in front of the army the next day. As the army went out for battle, God caused confusion among the attacking armies. They attacked each other, totally destroying themselves. For three days, Jehoshaphat and his soldiers carried off plunder from them. Then they returned to Jerusalem for a joyful celebration of the God's goodness and power. This event had a long-lasting impact on the king, the nation, and the surrounding countries. The Chronicler tells us, "The fear of God came on all the surrounding kingdoms when they heard how the LORD had fought against the enemies of Israel. And the kingdom of Jehoshaphat was at peace, for his God had given him rest on every side" (verses 29, 30).

> **God-inspired dreams always reflect our relationship with Him.**

In most conflicts, the armies of Israel got dirty and bloody carrying out the will of God. The account of the conquest of Canaan under Joshua shows that fulfilling God's dream is often difficult and costly. But this time, for this king, in this situation, God chose to work in a way that was beyond imagination. We can write our scripts of trust, praise, memories, and petition, but we can't dictate how God will direct our play. The uncertainties, however, don't have to overwhelm us and make us passive. We can see every day as a new scene in our play, one that requires planning and courage to p, but at every moment we must stay connected to the One who is our Supreme Creative Director.

Expert Planning

In *The Flawless Execution Model*,[3] James Murphy, a former F-15 fighter pilot, outlines a planning model with a simple but effective four-step process: plan, brief, execute, and debrief. Businesses and the military have used this model, but its principles apply to anyone who has a dream—in marriage, at work, in the family, or at church. Murphy's planning model is collaborative, involving every person who has a stake in the outcome. In the same way, we need to get input and buy-in from every person who is interested in the fulfillment of our dream. I want to adapt and apply these principles for our purposes.

Crafting the Plan

Steps of planning include:

Determine the objective: What will the dream look like when it's fulfilled? The picture of the outcome needs to be clear, measurable (if possible), and achievable (not too grandiose). We may envision a grand, sweeping goal, but it's wise to identify short-term goals that are impor-tant steps to get to the ultimate destination. By now, you probably have a good idea of what God's dream is for your life. God-inspired dreams always reflect our relationship with Him. We begin by saying, "Lord, I'm Yours. I offer myself as a living sacrifice. Lead me, use me, and empower me." With this relational foundation, we're assured that we're never alone as we pursue our dream.

Identify the obstacles: Some threats to our dreams are outside our control, but others are within our sphere of responsibility. Some are external, such as limited relationships or strained relationships, while others are internal, such as character defects or lack of skills. Quite frankly, one of the biggest obstacles to the dreams of many people is resentment. They're stuck in the past and can't envision anything in the future except, perhaps, revenge. We need to heal our past wounds so we don't carry them with us into the future. Then we can press on toward the upward call of God in Christ Jesus (Philippians 3:14). Similarly, we need to identify and change negative attitudes and bad habits so we can make progress toward the dream.

Identify resources: Quite often, people flounder in their lives because they haven't noticed all the resources available to them. I believe God has provided a wealth of resources in the people we know, the people we would know if introduced, training seminars or schools we could attend, books, and countless other helps. Invest in yourself. Take classes, find a mentor, go to seminars, and get professional certification and continued education. Always be a learner.

Absorb previous lessons: Like Jehoshaphat's reflection on God's past faithfulness, we can think back on previous experiences—good and bad—and evaluate the lessons we learn from them. We're wise to talk to family members and friends who were with us during those events. They often have a very different perspective.

Develop a clear, coherent plan: First, brainstorm ideas. Take the lid off your creativity and broaden your thinking to include everyone and everything possible. Then, gradually hone down the ideas to a few that are most promising. Compare them carefully, determine which looks most viable, and ask objective people for input. After receiving their feedback, fine-tune your plan—or start over. I recommend that people begin by going for small wins. If they shoot for big game and fail, many get discouraged and quit. Instead, set short-term and intermediate goals. As you make progress in reaching those, you gain confidence and develop new skills for bigger goals down the road. First, though, we need to taste success. For instance, a couple may want a restored, wonderful marriage, but their first goal might be to have a conversation without raising their voices, instead speaking a single, sincere word of affirmation. Or can they have one meal together without complaining about the job, the kids, or the in-laws.

Consider the "what ifs": Think about the roadblocks and contingencies that might arise. Like a pro quarterback who comes to the line and sees the defense lined up to stop the play called in the huddle, anticipate that you may need to call some audibles from time to time. Expect them, and be ready for them.

Brief

Your dream is about people, so you need to fully inform members of your family, work team, or committee about the plans you've developed. You asked for their input in the planning stage, but now that you've finalized your plan, explain it to them again. Paint a picture of the preferred future. What will the dream accomplish in people's lives? How will it shape everyone involved? Briefing people is part vision casting and part orientation to details. People have different temperaments. Some love bold vision but get bored with details. Others are suspicious of a vision that isn't backed by clear, specific plans, including the detailed responsibilities of everyone involved. If you have two or more people sitting at the table, assume that you have both kinds.

Execute the Plan

Murphy warns his readers against "task saturation," that is, having so many competing objectives to do that you lose sight of the major objective. One of the most useful (and commonly overlooked) tools in executing a plan is a detailed checklist. Almost every person who manages a project uses a checklist to stay on-task, identify lapses, and measure progress. Our God-given dream is no less important than building a house or selling widgets. (In fact, the dream may involve building houses and selling widgets.) Executing the plan includes enlisting the best efforts from every person involved. Leadership is both art and science. When we under-

Every good leader learns to light a fire of internal motivation in each person on the team.

stand the personalities and motivations of each person on the team or in the family, we can tailor our communication for maximum impact. A team spirit is essential. People may do what a dictator demands, but they won't like it, and they'll quit when the pressure is off. Every good leader learns to light a fire of internal motivation in each person on the team.

As the plan unfolds, it becomes complicated. People want to add objectives, sometimes competing objectives. If we're not careful, we lose the clear, compelling vision as the good ideas of others crowd our field of sight. Most of these ideas are very good ones. A wise leader discerns which complement the original vision and which ones obscure it.

Throughout the process, we need to keep going back to the Lord for wisdom and strength. Pilots call this "cross checking." I call it wisdom. We often need to get away from the noise of our lives so we can listen more intently to the Spirit's whisper, and while we're away, we regain emotional, spiritual, and relational perspective. We need to stay sharp to be able to handle the curveballs thrown at us. And there are always curveballs.

Debrief

After an event, the people who led it sometimes are so tired that they crawl into their cars and go home without thinking about it again. When we fail to debrief, we don't learn valuable lessons. For pilots, the failure to learn those lessons can cost them their lives the next time they go up.

For the rest of us, we can learn how to do every aspect of the planning model better so that we honor God more and accomplish His purposes more fully.

Objective feedback is essential in the debriefing process, but people may be too scared by their superiors to talk openly. When the Blue Angels, the Navy's Flight Demonstration Squadron, complete a show, the pilots and ground crew go into a room and close the door. A pilot explained that the name tags come off and the stripes on the shoulders are removed. Everyone shares without fear of retribution. Everyone shares in the mistakes.[4] Instead of protecting a fragile reputation or insisting on being right, people in this atmosphere are able to be open and honest. When they come out of the room, they are united in their purpose, no matter what was said in the debriefing. The attitude is, "It doesn't matter who made a mistake. Let's fix it together."

Do you see how you can use this planning model to fulfill your dreams? Some of us read this chapter and thought, "Where has this been? I love this, and I'll implement it today." But some responded differently: "This seems so constricting. I just want to trust God and watch Him work." Planning isn't used *instead* of trusting God; rather, it *is* trusting God to give us wisdom, direction, courage, and resources to do what He has called us to do.

New Pages in the Script

For years after I graduated, I enjoyed partnering with God in writing my dreams. Year after year, the plot unfolded as I pursued my ministry career. However, when I was asked to take a significant role in the financial administration of my denomination, I realized that I needed to develop new skills beyond the relational abilities and communication talents I had used for years. Since I began my new role, I've read books, talked to mentors, and attended specific seminars to learn the technical skills of managing corporate finances. As I've grown, I've used my previous skill-set, too, so I lost nothing, but I gained much in the transition. I never thought God would lead me into a role like this, but now I can see that He had His hands all over it.

For me, the new pages in the script seem to come fast and furiously. Not long ago, our daughter Ashley married a wonderful young man named John David—J.D. for short. On that day, my role changed. I was no longer the number one man in her life. Thankfully, I realized that fact, and I stepped into the role of an older peer who could give input—but only when she or he asked for it. If I played the "Dad card" and insisted on dictating Ashley's course of action like I did when she was a little girl, I would have damaged the relationship. The burden to change was on me, not them. I had to recognize the shift in our family's tectonic plates and adjust my expectations and communication accordingly. Today, my dream for Ashley is to see her and J.D. become strong and independent. I want to be there when they want my input and affirm them every step of the way, but mostly, I want to stay out of their way and let them thrive.

As Gail and I become empty nesters, her script is changing. For over twenty years, Gail has devoted her life to providing a safe, healthy, and fun environment for our girls. She poured herself into their lives, and she loved every minute of it. Now, I'm watching as she catches her breath and decides how she wants to invest the rest of her life. Gail has tremendous wisdom, so I increasingly bring her into my world to give input to me, our team, and the people we impact. For years, our lives revolved around the girls, so we're making adjustments in our communication. The change is great.

Don't be surprised by this vacillation. It's entirely normal. In fact, it's very productive because it shows creativity.

Transitions to different life-stages bring opportunities and challenges. Now that our girls have left home, Gail and I are reexamining our dreams in many different areas. Where do we want our finances to be when we're sixty? What does Gail want to do with her nurse's training and certification? When (and if) our daughters have children, what kind of margins does she need to be the grandmother she wants to be? Many of the new pages in our scripts are about enjoying each other.

Pick Up Your Pen

As you think about writing the script of your dream, consider three significant stages: the first draft, the edits, and the celebration.

The first draft: When people begin to think about God's dream, they dart in many different directions—sometimes in the same day. Young people have their hearts set on being a doctor, then a missionary, then a carpenter. Don't be surprised by this vacillation. It's entirely normal. In fact, it's very productive because it shows creativity. Identifying and clarifying God's dream isn't always easy. In most cases, it's like watching a Polaroid picture develop. Out of the darkness an image gradually becomes clearer. For people in this stage, trial and error are important. They take a stab at this job or that ministry, and they find they really like it or don't like it at all. Even more, they find that God uses them in a wonderful way, or what they're doing seems boring, difficult, and meaningless. As they begin to clarify the dream, they get additional training to sharpen their focus and acquire important skills, especially for a career. By the time they've written the first draft of their dream, they feel confident they're on the right path with God and they're beginning to see real results from their efforts.

The edits: Every playwright will tell you that the first draft is an endangered animal. Every reader takes a shot at it, offering advice and giving critiques. The editing process is crucial, though, because it shows how the script is uniquely crafted to tell a story in all its power and passion. In the same way, our dreams are edited in the middle part of our lives. They seldom change completely. More often, we craft this part and tailor that aspect so that it fits us just right. We handle the inevitable setbacks, learn from them, and press on to the next stage. Sometimes, the transition from the birth to the death of a dream occurs between the first draft and the edits, and its resurrection enables us to make substantial edits so that the dream has even more punch than before. In this stage, too, we often find the temptation of task saturation. We need to carefully evaluate so that we retain the things that are important, eliminate the good things that aren't essential, and shape our schedules and budgets around our finely tuned dream.

The party: The edits enable us to be successful and wise in following God's dream. As we see the dream unfold, we look back to celebrate and look forward to equip the next generation. We have lots of memories. We thank God for all He has allowed us to do, all He has given us, and all He has forgiven. We laugh at great memories, and we cry over our losses along the way. We've failed many times, but we have assurance of God's kindness and appreciation for everything we did for His honor. One of the joys of this stage is passing the torch to the next generation. We may or may not be able to pass on a pot of money, but we can pass on love, wisdom, hope, and stories of God's faithfulness to us. Those mean a lot more than gold.

Writing the script of our dreams is a challenge, but as we see it played out, we are thrilled that God uses us—even us!—to touch people's lives.

What's Your Take?

1. Where are you on the spontaneity-planning scale? What are the strengths and weaknesses of your approach?

2. Jehosaphat's dream was to build a strong, godly, safe kingdom. How did he respond to the threat from three armies? What lessons can you draw from his example?

3. How would you define and describe your dream today? How has it changed (if at all) since you answered the questions at the end of Chapter 1?

4. What are the current threats (under your control or not, external or internal)? What are your available resources to meet these threats?

5. How much are others in your life on board with your dream? Explain your answer.

6. How can you tell if you're letting too many priorities crowd out your dream? What can you do about it?

7. Do you expect to always be writing new pages for your script? Why or why not?

8. Which stage of playwriting are you in right now? How can you tell?

9. What do you need to write the next draft of your story?

Prayer of Commitment

Jesus, You continually unfold Your dream for me. I want to be alert, and I want to take advantage of every resource You've given me. Give me wisdom to lean not on my own understanding, but acknowledge You in all my ways, so that Your dream becomes clarified, and I don't miss a thing. Amen.

9 Passing the Dream On

The beginning of love is to let those we love be perfectly themselves, and not to twist them to fit our own image. Otherwise we love only the reflection of ourselves we find in them.

—Thomas Merton

Sometimes, the impact we have on others comes from a spontaneous act of kindness. Henry Moorehouse lived in a London slum in the 1800s. As he walked home one night, he saw a little girl carrying a pitcher full of milk. Suddenly, she fell and dropped the pitcher. It shattered in a hundred pieces, and she instantly burst into tears.

Moorehouse was moved with compassion. He told her gently, "Honey, don't cry."

Between gasps for breath, the little girl replied, "I'll get a whipping from my mommy."

"No, you won't," Moorehouse assured her. "I'll help you put the pitcher back together again."

With the assurance of a kind stranger, the girl stopped crying. Moorehouse gathered up the broken pieces of the pitcher, bought some glue, and began putting it together. Several times, it appeared he would succeed, but the pitcher fell apart again. After multiple failed attempts to fix the pitcher, the girl broke into tears again.

Moorehouse's heart broke as he watched her cry. He picked her up, took her to a store, and bought her a new pitcher. He then escorted her to another store to fill it with milk. Then he walked her to her home in the slum. At the door, Moorehouse asked the girl if she thought her mother would still spank her.

"No sir," she smiled. "This pitcher is much nicer than the one we had before."[1]

Sometimes, however, our impact is the result of studied resolve. A few years ago, on April Fool's Day, Gary Hamlin, a Missouri physician, decided that he would become a self-professed "fool for Christ." With remarkable self-awareness and humility, he said to himself, "I have lived the first forty years of my life for personal gain; now I want to start living for God." The doctor began to do seemingly foolish things. He invested his time and money to establish a center for troubled teenagers, he gave his services free of charge to a clinic for battered women and children, and he decided to become more involved in missions projects, planning eventually to close his practice and go to Haiti as a full-time medical missionary.

Since making this commitment, Hamlin said, "Materialism has lost its value. God was weaning me from the world's attractions. He was showing me His vision for my life. To be a fool for Him every day, but realize how rich I am."[2]

Leaving a Legacy

Every person on the planet leaves a legacy—for good or bad. We may think of retired people reflecting back on their lives to consider the impact they've had on others, but I believe we are wired to evaluate our influence at all stages of life. Even young people think about it. Junior high kids may be too self-absorbed to consider their impact on others, but by the time they graduate from high school, most teenagers look around them to see what kind of dent they've made in their friends and underclassmen. Young adults seek their own future in marriage and a career, but when they have kids, a "legacy gene" kicks in, and they begin to live for their kids' future. Adults in mid-life are well aware of the impact they've had on shaping the lives of their children. Some believe the mistakes they've made are irreparable, and it's too late to have a positive influence. But it's never too late.

What kind of legacy do we leave behind at every stage of our lives? As I watch people in families, business, friendships, and church, I see three kinds of legacies: We exasperate people, ignore them, or inspire them. I've seen people grit their teeth and shake their heads as they talk about parents, bosses, or church leaders. It's all these people can do to survive under the critical eye of those leaders. I've also seen the pain in people's eyes as they talked about being emotionally or physically abandoned by those who were supposed to care for them. Quite often, this happens in families when one or both parents die, leave in a divorce, or are physically present but emotionally absent. Sadly, the wound from being ignored doesn't have much shape, so it's harder to identify and resolve. But I've seen countless men and women, young and old, who point to a parent, teacher, employer, youth volunteer, or pastor and say, "You have no idea what this person has meant in my life. My life will never be the same because of them."

To pass the dream on to those around us, I believe we need four character qualities: empathy, modeling, faith, and hope. Let's look at those:

Empathy

One of the most important ways to connect with people is to show genuine empathy. This quality doesn't just acknowledge their experiences, it enters their feelings. We don't stand on the outside, make pronouncements, and give advice. Instead, we "get under the rock" with them so they know we understand, we care, and we're there for them.

Tolerating people isn't enough. Sometimes, all we offer others when they struggle is a shrug and a look that says, "I told you that wouldn't work." To have a powerful, positive impact on people, we need to do better than that. Where does authentic love come from? Jesus didn't tolerate us. He didn't look at our sins and flaws and shake His head in disgust. He entered our world, took the form of a servant, and gave himself to the point of death. The measure of love is the degree of sacrifice, and Christ gave all. The writer to the Hebrews tells us that Christ's empathy for us opens the door to a wonderful, close, supportive relationship. He wrote:

> *For we do not have a high priest who is unable to empathize with our weaknesses, but we have one who has been tempted in every way, just as we are—yet he did not sin. Let us then approach God's throne of grace with confidence, so that we may receive mercy and find grace to help us in our time of need (Hebrews 4:15,16).*

In the same way, when people are convinced we care, they open the door of their lives for us to impart God's mercy and grace when they're in need. What does it mean for us to become more like Christ? It means many things, but surely one of them is that we follow His example of imparting love, kindness, and hope to those around us. We may not fully comprehend what a person thinks, but we strive to grasp the depth of their emotions.

Do people know we really love them? Are we safe for them to be open and honest, or do we always have to fix them, blame them, and control them?

Modeling

One of the truths of human experience is that people are watching. Voyeurism is a deplorable sin, but to some degree, we're all keen observers of those around us. We read biographies of famous people; scour the news to find out what's going on in the lives of celebrities in sports, business, and entertainment; and we love to hear what's going on in each other's lives. We naturally long for connections, and like a duckling that is imprinted by watching its mother, our lives are powerfully shaped by those around us—and we shape theirs.

People watching everything we do. An intern at work observes how we display particular skills. Friends listen as we explain our views on anything and everything. Our children watch our every move and copy us like those ducklings copy their moms. Spouses even start to look like each other as time goes by. Teaching is important, but nothing is as powerful as modeling. I've talked to men and women in their later years who say that the influence of an adult (often, but not always their parents) in their formative years shaped their entire life.

People are watching what we do, but even more, they intuitively sense the nature of our character. They observe how we handle stress, how we treat the powerful and the weak, how we work, and whether our actions match our words. Today, people look beneath the surface to see if we are authentic. They still want to see *how* we do things, but even more, they want to know *why* we do those things. In fact, people today are very suspicious of anyone who claims to have all the answers. There are plenty of times when my girls see me struggle with an issue, and I tell them, "Pray for me. I don't know the right way to go, but I'm trusting God to show me."

The Philippians saw Paul be thrown into prison when a riot broke out after he cast a demon out of a girl. In the bowels of the dungeon, he and Silas sang praises to God, and the Lord shook the doors off the cell with an earthquake (Acts 16:16–40). In the full range of life's circumstances, from the glorious to the heartbreaking, the believers in Philippi had seen Paul walk with Christ. In his letter to them, he encouraged them by saying, "Whatever you have learned or received or heard from me, or seen in me—put it into practice. And the God of peace will be with you" (Philippians 4:9).

Are we people worth following? Are we modeling skills, or are we also giving others an example of noble and courageous character?

Faith

People are desperate to find believers whose faith is real. They've seen many go through the motions of being religious but without a foundation of vibrant trust in God, and they're turned off by the phoniness. How can they tell? When times are good, it's hard to tell what someone really believes, but in tough circumstances, real faith shines like a beacon. Faith is a conundrum—it's incredibly simple, yet amazingly complex. A child can exercise pure and powerful faith, but sometimes a seasoned believer has to dig deep through the mud of life to find God as a rock. The Scriptures encourage us to trust God in difficult times. The many names of God point us to different attributes of His majesty, love, and protection. Jesus exemplified ultimate trust in the Father when He drank the cup of wrath He didn't deserve to rescue us who richly deserved it.

In our walk with Christ, we experience priceless blessings and piercing heartaches. If the life of Jesus shows us both, can we expect anything else? In *Reaching for the Invisible God*, Philip Yancey states, "Gregory of Nicea once called St. Basil's faith 'ambidextrous' because he welcomed pleasures with the right hand and afflictions with the left, convinced that both would serve God's design for him."[3] God's gracious gifts of love, plenty, and happiness show us that He is generous and kind, but His purpose for our struggles is no less worthy. We, like St. Basil, need to gain a fresh perspective on our trials, suffering, and the delays we endure so that we are convinced that they, too, are part of God's loving plan for our lives. If we believe this, we, too, will rejoice in our troubles. And that will show we are growing in our ability to trust the greatness and grace of God when we don't see His hand at work—or when what we see is the opposite of what we expected. Both joy and sorrow are integral parts of being God's man or God's woman. After all, they were integral parts of the Savior's experience, too. And those around us are watching carefully to see if we'll trust God in the valleys as well as on the mountaintops.

Is our trust in God trouble-tested and strong? Do people see us with double-handed faith?

Hope

Sometimes I'm with believers who act like God has sentenced them to prison in this life. They complain, gripe, and whine about everything wrong in the world. They don't seem to remember the hope God gives in this life and in the one to come. No matter what happens to us, our experiences today are meaningful, not because we're so sharp or smart or good-looking, but because God is willing to use every triumph and tragedy for good—if we'll trust Him. And even if

I'd be in trouble if my hope was centered on me.

our lives are difficult today, and some of us endure immeasurable tragedies and chronic pain, God is preparing us for a glorious future with Him.

When I look back at my own life, I'm certain God knew exactly what He was doing when He brought me into the world at that time, in that family, and in those circumstances. I don't shake my fist at Him because my father died when I was a child. For a long time, I struggled with it, but after a while, God gave me insight about His kindness, wisdom, and sovereignty. "My hope," as the old song says, "is built on nothing less than Jesus Christ and His righteousness." It's not a function of my abilities and goodness. I'd be in trouble if my hope was centered on me. But Jesus is my hope—today, tomorrow, and for all eternity. I'm not enduring a prison sentence here; I'm enjoying a dress rehearsal of knowing, loving, and serving Christ that will be played out in the age to come.

Hope is a bedrock of trust in God's plans for our future. Without it, we disintegrate into despair and depression. But with it, we have the spark of life. We're creative, spontaneous, and joy-filled. We laugh, we love, and we aren't devastated by the problems that creep into our lives or explode upon them.

People need to see "hope with skin on" when they see us. As they watch our faces, do they see looks of eager anticipation in times of confusion and difficulty, or do they see grimaces of doubt? As they listen, do they hear words of confidence in the goodness and greatness of God, or do they hear grumbling and blaming others for our problems? We often quote the verse, "Taste and see that the LORD is good" (Psalm 34:8). When people taste us, what flavor do they experience? If all they hear from us are bland and meaningless platitudes, they'll look somewhere else. We need to share a clear-eyed grasp of reality, injected with a powerful trust in God's character and good plans for our lives. A hope-filled perspective doesn't imply that we have it all figured out, but we hold on tight to the One who does.

Do people around me know I love life? Are they convinced that I'm certain that God's plans are good and right, even if they look bad today? Does my hope in the future translate into joy, creativity, and laughter today?

Connections

Earlier, I mentioned that my parents threw me a catchable pass. They gave me the qualities I'd need for a lifetime, and they gave them in a way I could grasp. My dad was a wonderful man, full of love and life. He delighted in the Lord and in his family. I wish I could have had more years with him. And my mom was a stalwart of faith. She absorbed one of the most devastating blows anyone can experience. On all the psychological stress scales, the death of a child is the only event that is more crushing than the death of a spouse. She could have withdrawn into a world of self-pity, but she didn't. She could have become bitter and lashed out at God, me, and anyone who had it better than her, but she didn't. Day after day, she trusted God with her pain, found joy in everyday events, and modeled a vibrant spiritual life for her kids. I'll never forget how she passed the dream along to me.

But my mom and dad weren't the only people who had an impact on me. Bill Leach was our youth pastor when my dad died, and later he became pastor of the church. Bill was a wonderful father figure and mentor to me. I watched him like a hawk, and he consistently demonstrated a calm, proactive response to situations. He never panicked, and he was never passive. He looked at each situation with honesty and faith, and he took action that was appropriate time after time. And no matter how crazy I acted during those years, he loved me. Today, Bill and I are ministry colleagues. He is a treasured friend and still a strong, spiritual father whose character and counsel I highly respect.

Through some kind of spiritual osmosis, Bill's character sank into me, and I've tried to love my girls the same way Bill loved me. The message is, "There's absolutely nothing you can do that will cause me to stop loving you. Period. You can count on it." To be honest, I'm a control freak. I want everything to be exactly the way I think it ought to be, so my daily choice to affirm, accept, and be patient goes against my nature. The choice, though, has paid huge dividends. I think our daughters would say they can talk to Gail and me about anything. Nothing is off limits, including their dad trying to control everything. No matter what they say and do, Gail and I have chosen to respond with patience and love instead of reacting with shock and control. I hope we've modeled genuine faith, hope and love.

For the last several decades, I've wanted to throw a catchable pass to my girls. In all the interactions for the years they've lived under our roof, I've tried to impart this message in a thousand ways: "Your life matters to God, and He has given you incredible abilities to invest in the lives of others." I've tried to help them answer four crucial questions:

What's the *center* of your life?
What's the *contribution* of your life?
What's the *communication* of your life?
And what's the *character* of your life?

I long for them to know God's purpose for their lives, and I want them to revel in fulfilling it—free from guilt motivation, free from comparing themselves to others, and free from looking over their shoulders in doubt about God's leading. During the almost twenty years the girls were in our home, Gail and I were coaches and cheerleaders. We threw them passes every day. Sometimes they dropped them and had to learn how to catch them the next time, but quite often, they caught what we threw them. When they did, we cheered like they won a championship—but not too much because that would be hokey.

One of the most important passes I threw them was the importance of confession and repentance. From time to time, I failed to love them the way I should. When that happened, I sat down with them, often on the floor so we could be eyeball to eyeball. I told them that what I had done or said was wrong, and I asked them to forgive me—no excuse, no rationalization, and no minimizing. They watched Gail and me process tragedies, family relationships, and career choices. In the uncertainties of life, including living in a down economy, I wanted them to see us trust God for wisdom about how to handle our money. Even in tough times, we see every dime as a gift from God and celebrate His goodness to us.

Don't Just Take My Word for It

I've asked Gail and our two girls to explain how Gail and I have tried to help them find and follow God's dream for their lives.

From Gail . . .

The most important things I wanted to pass on to our girls were a love for God and a desire to live for Him and trust Him in all areas of their lives. As we all know, life can throw us curves that we have no control over, but I wanted more than anything for Ashley and Kaylee to have confidence that God would work everything out for their good.

Our girls are very different in a lot of ways, but one common theme that seemed hard for both of them to grasp was that God had a wonderful plan for their lives, and that if they would just trust in Him, He would lead them down the path to a more perfect future than they could ever imagine. Our girls were as different as sisters can be, but I loved their uniqueness. I saw such beauty, strength, and talent in both of them, and I wanted to make sure they knew that God had made them exactly the way He had planned —perfect!

Helping them grow into strong young women wasn't always easy, and at times it took very different parenting skills. I always desired for them to embrace who they were and appreciate each other's qualities. I wanted Ashley and Kaylee to know Doug and I were their biggest fans. No, they didn't always make the right decisions or choose the things we would have desired. As a result there were times of pain for all of us, but I wanted them to know that those choices never changed the love we had for them. It never changed our belief in them and God's plan for their futures. We always saw them as we knew they could be: beautiful woman of God with a purpose. We dedicated them to God as babies and trusted Him to bring them through whatever was happening in their lives to who they are today—the two most beautiful and amazing daughters I ever could have hoped for.

From Ashley . . .

"The catchable pass." This is a phrase I've heard ALL of my life. Growing up, my dad and mom always talked about tossing me catchable passes in life. It wasn't until a few years ago that I fully understood what this meant, and even more recently I discovered my parents' dedication to making sure that I caught those passes. Perhaps the thing I am most grateful for is their perseverance. They persevered in passing me lessons about life no matter how much I was opposed to catching them. At times, I'm sure it seemed that I had turned my back, folded my arms, and closed my eyes tight to avoid their input at all costs. But Mom and Dad stuck with me. They prayed for me and with me, they modeled Christ to me at all times and in all circumstances, and they never found any decision that I made (no matter how dumb) so horrific that they stopped telling me how much they loved me.

After getting hit in the head one too many times by these passes, I learned it was better to try to catch them than to stand there and let them hit me. I am so grateful that my parents never quit on me. And aside from being my coaches, my parents also became my teammates, cheerleaders, and defensive line. As my teammates, they stood by me, helped me up when I fell, and walked me through the best and worst times of my life. As my cheerleaders, they supported every dream that I could imagine. And as my defensive line, they defended me against others, myself, and Satan's attacks by praying relentlessly for me. My parents were everything I needed them to be to win in life. As I look at my life now, the blessings that surround me are endless, and I owe this to the favor of God for His biggest blessing of all—parents who threw me a catchable pass.

From Kaylee . . .

I always kept my parents on their toes. Ashley claimed the role of the Golden Child, so I happily took the role of the Mischief Child. And boy did I play that role well! I wasn't always a fan of the catchable pass, especially when good ole' Doug and Gail dragged me out of a hookah bar (where people smoke Turkish water pipes) at age fifteen. But I eventually learned to start catching it as it was being passed, and I'm sure glad I did.

My parents were always my biggest fans, and this fact helped me develop a pretty good conscience, because I didn't want to disappoint them or let them down. My parents have been there to love me unconditionally when I didn't deserve it. They always took my side and went to bat for me against anyone, and they made sure that Ashley and I followed the will of God. By doing these things, they taught me that being a Christian doesn't mean you have to be perfect, and it doesn't mean you're going to have to live a boring life. When you're living under God's plan, life is an exciting and wonderful journey.

I thank my parents for showing me what a godly marriage looks like and giving me the tools I'll need to have my own successful and healthy marriage one day. I feel so blessed to have two of the greatest role models I know be my parents. I love you guys!

Paul's Pass

We often think of Paul as a tough guy. He traveled from city to city knowing he would receive a very mixed response: some trusted in Christ and became his brothers and sisters in the faith, but others wanted to kill him. Certainly, he was bold and tenacious, but if we only look at that side of him, we miss something very important: he loved people, and they knew it. We get glimpses of his heart from his letters, but perhaps even more, Luke gives us reports of people's response to Paul as he traveled. On his way back to Jerusalem after his third missionary journey, Paul met with church leaders from Ephesus. He thanked them for standing with him during difficult times of his life, and he warned them that they would endure hardships. He encouraged them to remain strong in their faith as they kept serving Christ with a beautiful blend of zeal and humility. Luke tells us what happened next:

> When Paul had finished speaking, he knelt down with all of them and prayed. They all wept as they embraced him and kissed him. What grieved them most was his statement that they would never see his face again. Then they accompanied him to the ship (Acts 20:36–38).

Yes, Paul was tough, but he was tender, too. Men who endure ridicule and persecution together find out what's really inside, and what the elders saw in Paul was genuine faith and love. They were heartbroken that they wouldn't see him again.

One of Paul's most trusted disciples was a young man named Timothy. Paul wrote two letters to him when the old apostle was a prisoner in Rome, and he described Timothy in his letter to the Philippians. Paul first explained the humility and sacrifice of Christ. He told his readers, "In your relationships with one another, have the same mindset as Christ Jesus" (Philippians 2:5). Then, as Exhibit A of this mindset, he told them about Timothy's example of humble sacrifice:

> I hope in the Lord Jesus to send Timothy to you soon, that I also may be cheered when I receive news about you. I have no one else like him, who will show genuine concern for your welfare. For everyone looks out for their own interests, not those of Jesus Christ. But you know that Timothy has proved himself, because as a son with his father he has served with me in the work of the gospel. I hope,

therefore, to send him as soon as I see how things go with me (Philippians 2:19–23).

Paul followed the example of Christ, and Timothy followed both their examples. Timothy wasn't actually Paul's son, but the kind of relationship they had was, in many ways, like a father and son. In our lives, God can use us to pass dreams along to different people around us—our families, for sure, but also people at work, in our neighborhoods, at church, and perhaps even in countries around the world. God is looking for men and women whose hearts are completely His. Are you that man or woman? Will you be? Find and follow your dream. It will lead you to the foot of the Cross, and then to the doorsteps of people who need Jesus. It will be the greatest adventure of your life. Don't miss it!

What's Your Take?

1. Who has thrown you a "catchable pass" of love, faith, and a great future? What impact has that person had on you?

2. If you stopped today, what kind of legacy would you leave behind? What kind do you want to leave?

3. Why is empathy so important in connecting with people? What happens with it? What happens without it?

4. As people watch you, do they see someone who is honest, who trusts God in difficulties, and has a strong, joyful hope about the future? Or do they see someone who is self-absorbed and pessimistic? How would those closest to you answer these questions about you?

5. Who are two or three people that God has put in your life for you to start the fire of God's dream in their lives? What do you need to do to make this a reality? What needs to change?

6. If you'd been Timothy and read what Paul wrote about you in his letter to the Philippians, how would you feel? How would you respond?

7. What are the most important things you've learned from reading this book and reflecting on the questions in each chapter?

8. What's your next step to live God's dream in 3D?

Prayer of Commitment

Lord Jesus, I know You want to use me in others' lives. Thank You that You've forgiven me for my failures and taught me from my mistakes. Without You, I'd have very little to share with those I love. Give me wisdom beyond myself, and confidence in You as I seek to throw a catchable pass to those I love. Thank You for the privilege of being Your instrument. Amen.

Endnotes

Chapter 1

1   Quoted in John C. Maxwell, *Put Your Dream to the Test: 10 Questions to Help You See It and Seize It* (Nashville: Thomas Nelson, 2011), xviii.

2   Rick Warren, *The Purpose Driven Life: What on Earth Am I Here For?* (Grand Rapids, MI: Zondervan, 2002), 18, emphasis in original.

3   Cited by Michael Spath, University of Saint Francis, Convocation Address, August 28, 2002, The Council of Independent Colleges, www.cic.edu/makingthecase

4   Søren Kierkegaard, *The Prayers of Kierkegaard*, Perry LeFebre, ed. (Chicago, University of Chicago, 1956), 147.

5   Os Guinness, *The Call: Finding and Fulfilling the Central Purpose of Your Life*, (Nashville: Thomas Nelson, 2003), 4, emphasis in original.

6   Bill Hybels, *Holy Discontent: Fueling the Fire that Ignites Personal Vision* (Grand Rapids, MI: Zondervan, 2007), 22.

7   Guinness, *The Call*, 45, emphasis in original.

8   Martin Luther, "The Babylonian Captivity of the Church," in *Selected Writings of Martin Luther: 1529–1546*, ed. Thomas G. Tappert (Minneapolis, MN: Fortress, 1967), 430.

9   J. I. Packer, *Knowing God*, (Downers Grove, IL: InterVarsity, 1973), 227.

Chapter 2

1   Brian Dakss, "Autistic Teen's Hoop Dreams Come True," CBS News, February 23, 2006, http://www.cbsnews.com/stories/2006/02/23/earlyshow/main1339324.shtml.

2   C. S. Lewis, *Mere Christianity*, foreword by Kathleen Norris (New York: HarperCollins, 2001), 128.

3   Augustine, *Confessions*, trans. Henry Chadwick (Oxford: Oxford University Press, 1991),
4   Quoted in Ravi Zacharias, *Can Man Live without God?* (Dallas: Word, 1994), 58.

5   Walker Percy, *The Second Coming* (New York: Picador, 1999), 93.

6   Charles J. Sykes, *A Nation of Victims: The Decay of the American Character* (New York: St. Martin's, 1992).

7   Daniel Yankelovich, *New Rules: Searching for Self-Fulfillment in a World Turned Upside Down* (New York: Bantam, 1982).

8   Linda Stone, "Continuous Partial Attention," accessed May 16, 2011, http://lindastone. net/qa/continuous-partial-attention/.

9   Philip D. Kenneson, *Life on the Vine: Cultivating the Fruit of the Spirit in Christian Community*, (Downers Grove, IL: InterVarsity, 1999), 47.

10   Isaac Watts, "When I Survey the Wondrous Cross," in *Hymns and Spiritual Songs* (London: Strahan, 1707), 289.

11   Jane Herman, "Stepping Up: Cool Shoes for a Cool Cause: Buy One and Someone in Need Gets One Free," *Vogue* (October 2006), 248, accessed May 16, 2011, http://cdn2.toms-shoes.com/images/uploads/2006-oct-vogue.jpg.

12   Martin Luther King Jr., *Strength to Love* (New York: Harper & Row, 1963), 35.

13   Quoted in John C. Maxwell, *Developing the Leader within You* (Nashville: Thomas Nelson, 1993), 45.

14   R. A. Torrey, *Why God Used D. L. Moody*, accessed May 16, 2011, http://www. wholesomewords.org/biography/biomoody6.html.

15   Oswald Chambers, "September 29th: The Consciousness of the Call," online edition of *My Utmost for His Highest*, accessed May 16, 2011, http://www.myutmost.org/09/0929.html.

Chapter 3

1   Martin Luther King Jr., "Overcoming an Inferiority Complex," accessed May 16, 2011, http://mlk-kpp01.stanford.edu/primarydocuments/Vol6/14July1957OvercominganInferiorit yComplex.pdf

Chapter 4

1   John A. Murray, "The Spiritual Pathway to March Madness," *Wall Street Journal*, March 8, 2011, http://online.wsj.com/article/SB10001424052748704131404575117742726044162. html

2   Augustine says that a righteous person "neither loves what he ought not to love, nor fails to love what he ought to love, nor loves that more which ought to be loved less, nor loves that equally which ought to be loved either less or more, nor loves that less or more which ought to

be loved equally." *On Christian Doctrine*, Book I, Chapter 27, accessed May 16, 2011, http://www.ccel.org/ccel/schaff/npnf102.v.iv.xxvii.html.

3   B. B. Warfield, "On the Emotional Life of Our Lord," accessed May 16, 2011, http://books.google.com/books?id=3edJAAAAMAAJ&printsec=titlepage#v=onepage&q&f=false.

4   Jack Johnson, "The News," *Brushfire Fairytales* (Brushfire Records, 2001).

5   Dr. Richard Swenson, *Margin: Restoring Emotional, Physical, Financial and Time Reserves to Our Overloaded Lives*, (Navpress, Colorado Springs, 2004).

6   Cited in Stephen E. Ambrose, *Band of Brothers*, (New York: Simon & Schuster, 2001), 203.

7   "The Mental Toll," in *The Perilous Fight: America's World War II in Color*, PBS.org, accessed on May 16, 2011, www.pbs.org/perilousfight/psychology/the_mental_toll/.

8   See NIV 1984 and 2011, respectively, for the *counselor* and *advocate*.

9   N. T. Wright, *After You Believe: Why Christian Character Matters* (New York: HarperOne, 2010), 106.

Chapter 5

1   Thomas Paine, *The Crisis*, December 23, 1776, accessed May 16, 2011, http://www.ushistory.org/paine/crisis/c-01.htm.

2   Lewis Smedes, *Forgive and Forget: Healing the Hurts We Don't Deserve* (New York: Harper & Row, 1984), 79.

3   Lewis Smedes, *The Art of Forgiving: When You Need To Forgive And Don't Know How* (New York: Ballantine, 1996), 171.

4   Transcribed from "Michael Jordan 'Failure' Nike Commercial," *YouTube*, accessed May 16, 2011, http://www.youtube.com/watch?v=45mMioJ5szc.

5   Quoted in "Climbing Mount Everest Is Work for Supermen," *New York Times*, March 18, 1923.

6   This story is from the biography of Stacy Allison, www.beyondthelimits.com, accessed May 18, 2011.

7   Stacy Allison, *Beyond the Limits: A Woman's Triumph on Everest* (City: Little Brown & Co, 1993); and *Many Mountains to Climb: Reflections on Competence, Courage and Commitment* (Bothell, WA: Hara Publishing Group, 1999).

8   Stacy Allison, "About Stacy," www.beyondthelimits.com, accessed May 18, 2011.

Chapter 6

1   Amber Hensley, "10 Big Differences Between Men's and Women's Brains," Master Healthcare, last modified 16, 2009, accessed May 16, 2011, http://www.mastersofhealthcare.com/blog/2009/10-big-differences-between-mens-and-womens-brains/.

2   Shelley E. Taylor, "Tend and Befriend: Biobehavioral Bases of Affiliation under Stress," *Current Directions in Psychological Science*, 15 (December 2006): 273-277.

3   Robert Lewis, The Quest for Authentic Manhood, (LifeWay Christian Resources, 2005), a 24-week study.

4   Cited in *The Promise*, by Robert J. Morgan, (B&H Books, Nashville, 2008), 53.

Chapter 7

1   "Ben Comen's Inspirational Story of Running," Inspiring Sports Motivations, last modified November 8, 2010, accessed May 16, 2011, http://inspiringsportsmotivations.com/ben-comens.

2   Martin Luther, "Disputation on the Power and Efficacy of Indulgences Commonly Known as the 95 Theses," accessed May 17, 2011, http://www.spurgeon.org/~phil/history/95theses.htm.

3   C. S. Lewis, "The Weight of Glory," accessed May 16, 2011, www.verber.com/mark/xian/weight-of-glory.pdf

Chapter 8

2   *The Purpose Driven Life: What on Earth Am I Here For?*

3   *Flawless Execution: Use the Techniques and Systems of America's Fighter Pilots to Perform at Your Peak and Win the Battles of the Business*

4   *Flawless Execution*

Chapter 9

1   Adapted from *Grace Gone Wild: Getting A Grip On God's Amazing Gift* by Robert Jeffress, (Waterbrook Press, 2005).

2   Robert Jeffress, *The Solomon Secrets: 10 Keys to Extraordinary Success from Proverbs* (Colorado Springs, CO: WaterBrook, 2002), 12–13.

3   Philip Yancey, *Reaching for the Invisible God: What Can We Expect to Find?* (Grand Rapids, MI: Zondervan, 2000), 69.

About Doug Clay

Doug Clay serves as the General Treasurer for the General Council of the Assemblies of God. As a member of the Executive Leadership Team, he brings a clear vision and a strong passion for church health.

Doug firmly believes the church is the primary instrument God uses to expand His Kingdom here on earth. That's why he has devoted himself fully to the cause of resourcing ministries and churches for health and growth. His life and work are driven by the truth of Paul's insight written to the Christians in Ephesus: "For we are God's handiwork, created in Christ Jesus to do good works, which God prepared in advance for us to do" (2:10). Clay's chief goal in life is to help people realize their God-given dreams.

Each Monday, Doug shares his thoughts on life and leadership through "Monday Motivator," a video blog that can be seen at http:// agtv.ag.org/monday-motivator. He loves life and people. He often tells his audience that God has not sentenced us to life as something to endure, but to enjoy, and to enjoy it with others!

Prior to taking office as the General Treasurer, Doug served as superintendent of the Ohio Ministry Network from June 2004 to 2008. He was pastor of Calvary Assembly of God in Toledo, Ohio, from 1997 to 2004. He has also served as the Assemblies of God national youth director (1995-1997), Ohio District youth director (1989-1995) and as a youth pastor in Ohio and Iowa.

Doug and his wife, Gail, have two daughters and a son-in-law. He enjoys golf, racquetball, reading and sharing a latte with friends.

Follow Clay on Twitter (@DougClay) or you can find him on Facebook.

Leading a Group or Class Using *Dreaming in 3D*

This book is designed for individual study, small groups, and classes. The best way to absorb and apply these principles is for each person to individually study and answer the questions at the end of each chapter, then to discuss them in either a class or a group environment.

Each chapter's questions are designed to promote reflection, application, and discussion. Order enough copies of the book for everyone to have a copy. For couples, encourage both to have their own book so they can record their individual reflections.

A recommended schedule for a small group might be:

Week 1: Introduce the material. As a group leader, tell your story of finding and fulfilling God's dream, share your hopes for the group, and provide books for each person. Encourage people to read the assigned chapter each week and answer the questions.

Weeks 2–10: Each week, introduce the topic for the week and share a story of how God has used the principles in your life. In small groups, lead people through a discussion of the questions at the end of the chapters. In classes, teach the principles in each chapter, use personal illustrations, and invite discussion.

Personalize Each Lesson

Don't feel pressured to cover every question in your group discussions. Pick out three or four that had the biggest impact on you, and focus on those, or ask people in the group to share their responses to the questions that meant the most to them that week.

Make sure you personalize the principles and applications. At least once in each group meeting, add your own story to illustrate a particular point.

Make the Scriptures come alive. Far too often, we read the Bible like it's a phone book, with little or no emotion. Paint a vivid picture for people. Provide insights about the context of people's encounters with God, and help people in your class or group sense the emotions of specific people in each scene.

Focus on Application

The questions at the end of each chapter and your encouragement to group members to be authentic will help your group take big steps to apply the principles they're learning. Share how you are applying the principles in particular chapters each week, and encourage them to take steps of growth, too.

Three Types of Questions

If you have led groups for a few years, you already understand the importance of using open questions to stimulate discussion. Three types of questions are *limiting, leading,* and *open.* Many of the questions at the end of each day's lessons are open questions.

Limiting questions focus on an obvious answer, such as, "What does Jesus call himself in John 10:11?" These don't stimulate reflection or discussion. If you want to use questions like this, follow them with thought-provoking open questions.

Leading questions require the listener to guess what the leader has in mind, such as, "Why did Jesus use the metaphor of a shepherd in John

10?" (He was probably alluding to a passage in Ezekiel, but many people don't know that.) The teacher who asks a leading question has a definite answer in mind. Instead of asking this kind of question, you should just teach the point and perhaps ask an open question about the point you have made.

Open questions usually don't have right or wrong answers. They stimulate thinking, and they are far less threatening because the person answering doesn't risk ridicule for being wrong. These questions often begin with "Why do you think...?" or "What are some reasons that...?" or "How would you have felt in that situation?"

Preparation

As you prepare to teach this material in a group or class, consider these steps:

1. Carefully and thoughtfully read the book. Make notes, highlight key sections, quotes, or stories, and complete the reflection sections at the end of each day's chapter. This will familiarize you with the entire scope of the content.

2. As you prepare for each week's class or group, read the corresponding chapters again and make additional notes.

3. Tailor the amount of content to the time allotted. You won't have time to cover all the questions, so pick the ones that are most pertinent.

4. Add your own stories to personalize the message and add impact.

5. Before and during your preparation, ask God to give you wisdom, clarity, and power. Trust Him to use your group to change people's lives.

6. Most people will get far more out of the group if they read the chapters and complete the reflection each week. Order books before the group or class begins or after the first week.

To Order More Copies

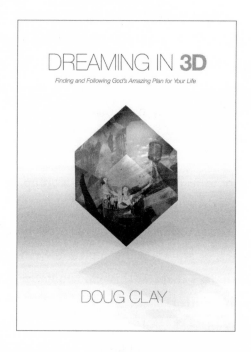

To order more copies of this book, go to

www.influence-resources.com